Grade 4

All images ©Houghton Mifflin Harcourt, Inc., unless otherwise noted
Cover: ©harryhayashi/iStock/Getty Images Plus

Copyright © by Houghton Mifflin Harcourt Publishing Company

All rights reserved. No part of this work may be reproduced or transmitted in any form or by any means, electronic or mechanical, including photocopying or recording, or by any information storage or retrieval system, without the prior written permission of the copyright owner unless such copying is expressly permitted by federal copyright law. Requests for permission to make copies of any part of the work should be submitted through our Permissions website at https://customercare.hmhco.com/contactus/Permissions.html or mailed to Houghton Mifflin Harcourt Publishing Company, Attn: Compliance, Contracts, and Licensing, 9400 Southpark Center Loop, Orlando, Florida 32819-8647.

Printed in the U.S.A.

ISBN 978-0-358-29936-3

3 4 5 6 7 8 9 10 0607 29 28 27 26 25 24 23 22 21

4500823715

r2.21

> If you have received these materials as examination copies free of charge, Houghton Mifflin Harcourt Publishing Company retains title to the materials and they may not be resold. Resale of examination copies is strictly prohibited.

> Possession of this publication in print format does not entitle users to convert this publication, or any portion of it, into electronic format.

Whose book is this?

Observe the cover.

I notice _____
_____

I wonder _____
_____

A scientist ...

is

can

uses

Design your own robot.

Science makes me feel ...

    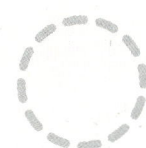

I like science because ... _____

_____

_____

_____

Consulting Authors

Michael A. DiSpezio
Global Educator
North Falmouth, Massachusetts

Marjorie Frank
Science Writer and Content-Area
  Reading Specialist
Brooklyn, New York

Michael R. Heithaus, PhD
Dean, College of Arts, Sciences &
  Education Professor, Department
  of Biological Sciences
Florida International University
Miami, Florida

Peter McLaren
Executive Director of Next Gen Education, LLC
Providence, Rhode Island

Bernadine Okoro
Social Emotional
Learning Consultant
STEM Learning Advocate & Consultant
Washington, DC

Cary Sneider, PhD
Associate Research Professor
Portland State University
Portland, Oregon

Program Advisors

Paul D. Asimow, PhD
Eleanor and John R. McMillan Professor of Geology and
  Geochemistry
California Institute of Technology
Pasadena, California

Eileen Cashman, PhD
Professor of Environmental Resources Engineering
Humboldt State University
Arcata, California

Mark B. Moldwin, PhD
Professor of Climate and Space Sciences and Engineering
University of Michigan
Ann Arbor, Michigan

Kelly Y. Neiles, PhD
Associate Professor
  of Chemistry
St. Mary's College of Maryland
St. Mary's City, Maryland

Sten Odenwald, PhD
Astronomer
NASA Goddard Spaceflight
  Center
Greenbelt, Maryland

Bruce W. Schafer
Director of K-12 STEM Collaborations, Retired
Oregon University System
Portland, Oregon

Barry A. Van Deman
President and CEO
Museum of Life and Science
Durham, North Carolina

Kim Withers, PhD
Assistant Professor
Texas A&M
  University-Corpus Christi
Corpus Christi, Texas

Classroom Reviewers

Julie Ahern
Andrew Cooke Magnet School
Waukegan, Illinois

Amy Berke
South Park Elementary School
Rapid City, South Dakota

Pamela Bluestein
Sycamore Canyon School
Newbury Park, California

Kelly Brotz
Cooper Elementary School
Sheboygan, Wisconsin

Andrea Brown
HLPUSD Science and STEAM TOSA, Retired
Hacienda Heights, California

Marsha Campbell
Murray Elementary School
Hobbs, New Mexico

Leslie C. Antosy-Flores
Star View Elementary School
Midway City, California

Theresa Gailliout
James R. Ludlow Elementary School
Philadelphia, Pennsylvania

Emily Giles
Assistant Principal
White's Tower Elementary School
Independence, KY

Robert Gray
Essex Elementary School
Baltimore, Maryland

Stephanie Greene
Science Department Chair
Sun Valley Magnet School
Sun Valley, California

Roya Hosseini
Junction Avenue K–8 School
Livermore, California

Rana Mujtaba Khan
Will Rogers High School
Van Nuys, California

George Kwong
Schafer Park Elementary School
Hayward, California

Kristin Kyde
Templeton Middle School
Sussex, Wisconsin

Marie LaCross
Sulphur Springs United School District
Santa Clarita, California

Bonnie Lock
La Center Elementary School
La Center, Washington

Imelda Madrid
Assistant Principal
Montague Charter Academy for the Arts and Sciences
Pacoima, CA

Susana Martinez O'Brien
Diocese of San Diego
San Diego, California

Kara Miller
Ridgeview Elementary School
Beckley, West Virginia

Mercy D. Momary
Local District Northwest
Los Angeles, California

Dena Morosin
Shasta Elementary School
Klamath Falls, Oregon

Craig Moss
Mt. Gleason Middle School
Sunland, California

Joanna O'Brien
Palmyra Elementary School
Palmyra, Missouri

Wendy Savaske
Education Consultant
Wisconsin Department of Public Instruction

Isabel Souto
Schafer Park Elementary School
Hayward, California

Michelle Sullivan
Balboa Elementary School
San Diego, California

April Thompson
Roll Hill School
Cincinnati, Ohio

Tina Topoleski
District Science Supervisor
Jackson School District
Jackson, New Jersey

Terri Trebilcock
Fairmount Elementary School
Golden, Colorado

Emily R.C.G. Williams
South Pasadena Middle School
South Pasadena, California

Engineering..xi
Claims, Evidence, and Reasoning.....................xiii
Safety in Science..xv

Unit 1 Engineering and Technology 1

Lesson 1 Engineering Design 2
- **HANDS ON** **Engineer It** Quick Tower Building 4
- **HANDS ON** **Engineer It** Designing a Listening Device 6

Unit Review 22

Unit 2 Plant and Animal Structure and Function 25

Lesson 1 **Plant Parts and How They Function** 26
- HANDS ON Flower Power 28
- HANDS ON Slurp! 32

Lesson 2 **Animal Parts and How They Function** 44
- HANDS ON Dinner Is Served 46
- HANDS ON Courtship Displays 50

Lesson 3 **How Senses Work** 64
- HANDS ON Touch Test 66
- HANDS ON No Smell, No Taste, No See 70

Unit Review 84

Unit 3 Energy and Communication 87

Lesson 1 Energy Transfer and Transformation 88
- **HANDS ON** Full of Energy 90
- **HANDS ON** Light the Bulb 94

Lesson 2 Collisions 108
- **HANDS ON** Test It! Stored Energy in a Rubber Band 110
- **HANDS ON** Speed and Energy 114

Lesson 3 Waves 124
- **HANDS ON** Let's Make Waves! 126
- **HANDS ON** Bobbing and Waving 129

Lesson 4 Information Transfer 142
- **HANDS ON** **Engineer It** Communication Solution 144
- **HANDS ON** Pixels to Pictures 147

Unit Review 162

Unit 4 Shaping Landforms 165

Lesson 1 Factors That Shape Earth's Surface 166
- HANDS ON Modeling How Far Sediment Travels 168
- HANDS ON A Sweet Test 171

Lesson 2 Fast and Slow Changes 182
- HANDS ON The Rate of Change 184
- HANDS ON Glaciers on the Move 188

Lesson 3 Rock Layers Record Landform Changes 198
- HANDS ON Layered Landforms 200
- HANDS ON Layer by Layer 202

Unit Review 218

What a view!

Unit 5 Earth's Features and Resources 221

Lesson 1 **Patterns on Earth** 222
- HANDS ON Tracking Quakes 224
- HANDS ON Volcanic Eruptions 228

Lesson 2 **Reducing the Impacts of Natural Hazards** 238
- HANDS ON **Engineer It** Strong, Stable Structures 240
- HANDS ON Make Your Own Seismograph 243

Lesson 3 **Resources** 256
- HANDS ON Modeling Energy Resource Use 258
- HANDS ON **Engineer It** Running on Sunshine 262

Unit Review 278

Interactive Glossary G1
Index I12

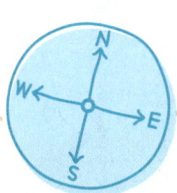

Engineering

Engineers develop solutions for all types of problems. Engineers use an engineering design process to help them find a good solution to a problem. They use this process to solve problems to meet people's wants and needs. One engineering design process is shown here.

This engineering design process has three main parts, or *phases*. You may use this three-phase process to solve many different types of problems.

EXPLORE

In the *Explore* phase, you learn more about the problem by asking questions and doing research. Can you think of other ways to learn more about a problem? After you have gathered information about the problem, you state the problem clearly. Then you identify what features a good solution should have. The desirable features of a solution are called **criteria**. You may also identify limits, or **constraints**, on an acceptable solution. The problem is defined when you've identified criteria and constraints and stated the problem clearly.

MAKE and TEST

In the *Make and Test* phase, you develop a good solution. This phase may include the following steps:

- Brainstorm
- Plan
- Design
- Test
- Evaluate

When you brainstorm, you think of as many ideas as you can. These ideas may or may not solve the problem you defined in the *Explore* phase. Use the criteria, constraints, and problem statement to choose which solutions you think will work best. Then you can plan and make a prototype to test. A **prototype** is a model of a solution that can be tested.

Testing a prototype helps you know how well a solution works. If a solution does not solve the problem, you may change the solution and test again. You must test a solution after each change so you know how well the changed solution works. You may also find out that you need to choose a different solution to make and test.

There may be more than one acceptable solution to a problem. Use test results to choose which solution is better. The solution that best meets the criteria and constraints is the better solution. Once you have found a good solution to solve the problem, you can move to the third phase, *Improve and Test*.

IMPROVE and TEST

In the *Improve and Test* phase, you do many of the same steps as the *Make and Test* phase. You may replan, redesign, and retest many small changes. You may even return to an earlier phase if needed. Throughout the process, you communicate with others to share information or learn more. At the end of the process, you should have as good a solution as possible, given the constraints. Your solution is ready to use or share with others.

Hana wants to attract pretty birds to her backyard. Talk with a partner about how Hana might use an engineering design process to solve this problem.

Claims, Evidence, and Reasoning

Constructing Explanations

A complete scientific explanation needs three parts—a claim, evidence, and reasoning.

A **claim** is a statement you think is true. A claim answers the question, "What do you know?" **Evidence** is data collected during an investigation. Evidence answers the question, "How do you know that?" **Reasoning** tells the connection between the evidence and the claim. Reasoning answers the question, "Why does your evidence support your claim?"

Suppose you're investigating what combination of baking soda and vinegar will produce the largest "volcanic" eruption. Specifically, you are increasing the amount of vinegar but leaving the amount of baking soda the same.

> The largest amount of vinegar will react the most.

You have three containers of vinegar—50 mL, 100 mL, and 200 mL—and one tablespoon of baking soda for each container. Before you begin, you make a **claim**.

Then you add the baking soda to each container and observe. The data you gather is your **evidence**. You can use data to show if your claim is true or not. Now you're ready to construct a scientific explanation with a claim, evidence, and reasoning.

Claim	I think the largest amount of vinegar will react the most.
Evidence	The container with 200 mL of vinegar made more bubbles than the containers with 50 mL and 100mL.
Reasoning	The evidence showed that more vinegar makes a larger reaction than a little vinegar.

Evidence used to support a claim can be used to make another claim.

You decide to try a different type of investigation. Describe it below, then record your possible claim, evidence, and reasoning.

My investigation is

Claim	
Evidence	
Reasoning	

Safety in the Lab

Doing science is a lot of fun. But, a science lab can be a dangerous place. Falls, cuts, and burns can happen easily. **Know the safety rules and listen to your teacher.**

- ☐ **Think ahead.** Study the investigation steps so you know what to expect. If you have any questions, ask your teacher. Be sure you understand all caution statements and safety reminders.
- ☐ **Be neat and clean.** Keep your work area clean. If you have long hair, pull it back so it doesn't get in the way. Roll or push up long sleeves to keep them away from your activity.
- ☐ **Oops!** If you spill or break something, or get cut, tell your teacher right away.
- ☐ **Watch your eyes.** Wear safety goggles anytime you are directed to do so. If you get anything in your eyes, tell your teacher right away.
- ☐ **Yuck!** Never eat or drink anything during a science activity.
- ☐ **Don't get shocked.** Be careful if an electric appliance is used. Be sure that electric cords are in a safe place where you can't trip over them. Never use the cord to pull a plug from an outlet.
- ☐ **Keep it clean.** Always clean up when you have finished. Put everything away and wipe your work area. Wash your hands.
- ☐ **Play it safe.** Always know where to find safety equipment, such as fire extinguishers. Know how to use the safety equipment around you.

Safety in the Field

Lots of science research happens outdoors. It's fun to explore the wild! But, you need to be careful. The weather, the land, and the living things can surprise you.

- ☐ **Think ahead.** Study the investigation steps so you know what to expect. If you have any questions, ask your teacher. Be sure you understand all caution statements and safety reminders.
- ☐ **Dress right.** Wear appropriate clothes and shoes for the outdoors. Cover up and wear sunscreen and sunglasses for sun safety.
- ☐ **Clean up the area.** Follow your teacher's instructions for when and how to throw away waste.
- ☐ **Oops!** Tell your teacher right away if you break something or get hurt.
- ☐ **Watch your eyes.** Wear safety goggles when directed to do so. If you get anything in your eyes, tell your teacher right away.
- ☐ **Yuck!** Never taste anything outdoors.
- ☐ **Stay with your group.** Work in the area as directed by your teacher. Stay on marked trails.
- ☐ **"Wilderness"** doesn't mean go wild. Never engage in horseplay, games, or pranks.
- ☐ **Always walk.** No running!
- ☐ **Play it safe.** Know where safety equipment can be found and how to use it. Know how to get help.
- ☐ **Clean up.** Wash your hands with soap and water when you come back indoors.

Safety Symbols

To highlight important safety concerns, the following symbols are used in a Hands-On Activity. Remember that no matter what safety symbols you see, all safety rules should be followed at all times.

Dress Code

- Wear safety goggles as directed.
- If anything gets into your eye, tell your teacher immediately.
- Do not wear contact lenses in the lab.
- Wear appropriate protective gloves as directed.
- Tie back long hair, secure loose clothing, and remove loose jewelry.

Glassware and Sharp Object Safety

- Do not use chipped or cracked glassware.
- Notify your teacher immediately if a piece of glass breaks.
- Use extreme care when handling all sharp and pointed instruments.
- Do not cut an object while holding the object in your hands.
- Cut objects on a suitable surface, always in a direction away from your body.

Electrical Safety

- Do not use equipment with frayed electrical cords or loose plugs.
- Do not use electrical equipment near water or when clothing or hands are wet.
- Hold the plug when you plug in or unplug equipment.

Chemical Safety

- If a chemical gets on your skin, on your clothing, or in your eyes, rinse it immediately, and tell your teacher.
- Do not clean up spilled chemicals unless your teacher directs you to do so.
- Keep your hands away from your face while you are working on any activity.

Heating and Fire Safety

- Know your school's fire-evacuation routes.
- Never leave a hot plate unattended while it is turned on or while it is cooling.
- Allow equipment to cool before storing it.

Plant and Animal Safety

- Do not eat any part of a plant.
- Do not pick any wild plant unless your teacher instructs you to do so.
- Treat animals carefully and respectfully.
- Wash your hands throughly after handling any plant or animal.

Cleanup

- Clean all work surfaces and protective equipment as directed by your teacher.
- Wash your hands throughly before you leave the lab or after any activity.

Safety Quiz

Name _____

Circle the letter of the BEST answer.

1. At the end of any activity, you should
    a. wash your hands thoroughly before leaving the lab.
    b. cover your face with your hands.
    c. put on your safety goggles.
    d. leave the materials where they are.

2. If you get hurt or injured in any way, you should
    a. tell your teacher immediately.
    b. find bandages or a first aid kit.
    c. go to your principal's office.
    d. get help after you finish the activity.

3. Before starting an activity, you should
    a. try an experiment of your own.
    b. open all containers and packages.
    c. read all directions and make sure you understand them.
    d. handle all the equipment to become familiar with it.

4. When working with materials that might fly into the air and hurt someone's eye, you should wear
    a. goggles.
    b. an apron.
    c. gloves.
    d. a hat.

5. If you get something in your eye, you should
    a. wash your hands immediately.
    b. put the lid back on the container.
    c. wait to see if your eye becomes irritated.
    d. tell your teacher right away.

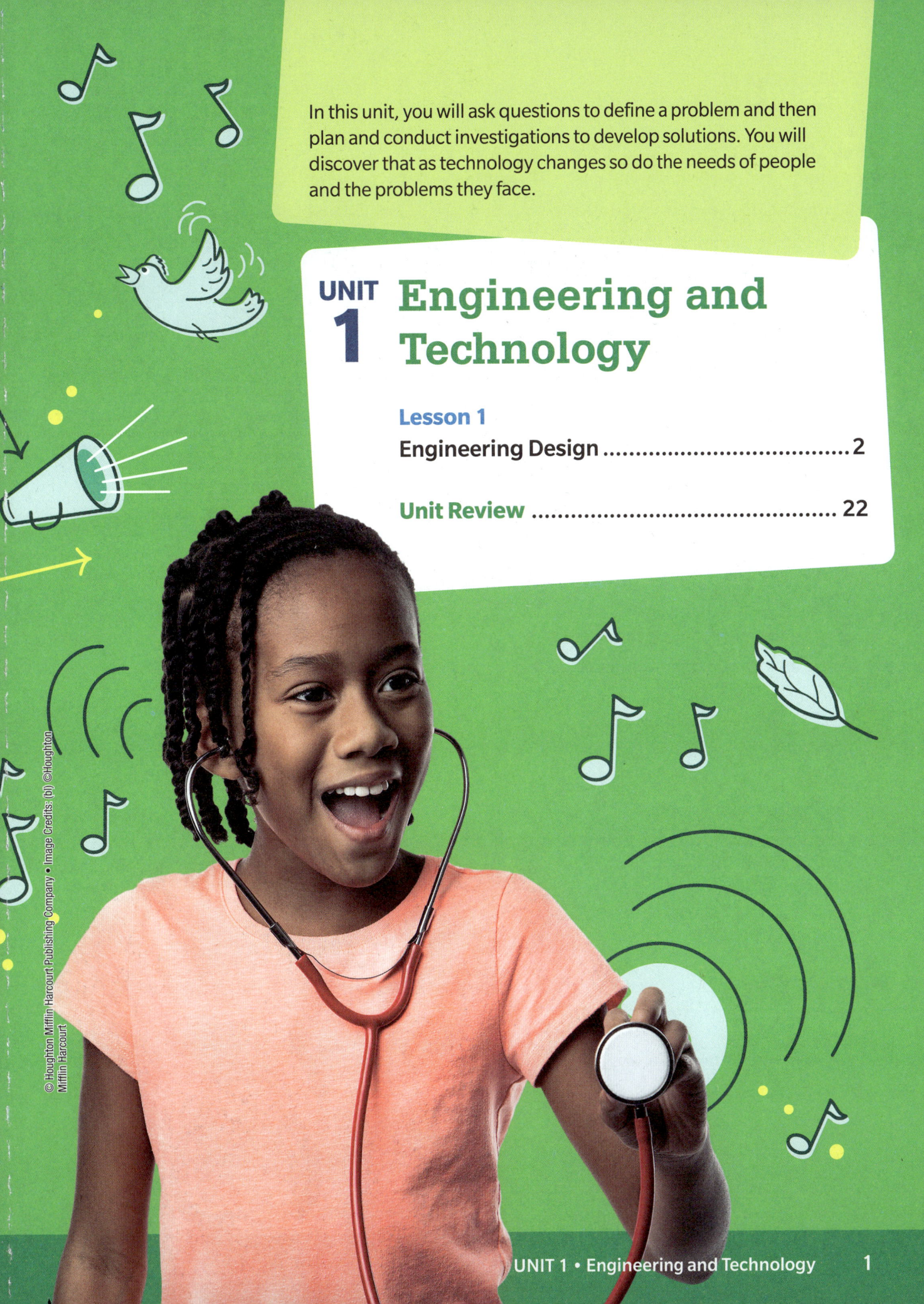

In this unit, you will ask questions to define a problem and then plan and conduct investigations to develop solutions. You will discover that as technology changes so do the needs of people and the problems they face.

UNIT 1 Engineering and Technology

Lesson 1
Engineering Design 2

Unit Review 22

What do you notice about what this person is doing?

I notice _____

_____

_____

_____

What do you wonder about what this person is doing?

I wonder _____

_____

_____

_____

Can You Solve It?

How can you design and build a lightweight, nonelectric listening device to use on a nature walk? Sketch, write, or model your answer.

HANDS-ON ACTIVITY

Engineer It
Quick Tower Building

Engineers solve problems to meet people's wants and needs. Their solutions must meet certain criteria. **Criteria** are desirable features of a solution. In addition to meeting criteria, engineers have to make sure their solutions meet the constraints. A **constraint** is a limit on possible solutions, such as cost or materials. In this activity, you will be challenged to build the tallest structure you can that will not fall over. You can only use 10 sheets of construction paper and 30 cm of tape.

Form a question Ask a question about how criteria and constraints are involved in developing design solutions.

Did you know?
The tallest building is the Burj Khalifa in Dubai. It is 829.8 m (2,722 ft) tall!

LESSON 1 • **Engineering Design**

POSSIBLE MATERIALS

☐ 10 sheets of construction paper   ☐ 30 cm of tape

Make and Test

Design a solution You have 10 sheets of paper and 30 cm of tape. In 10 minutes, work as a team to build the tallest structure you can that won't fall over and that can support the weight of one book.

Identify the criteria and constraints. Which were the hardest to meet?

_____

_____

_____

_____

Draw conclusions Did your design meet the goals of this activity? Support your **claim** with **evidence** and **reasoning.**

_____

_____

_____

_____

With a partner, discuss two examples of good communication and teamwork that you followed during this investigation.

Making Sense

How does your claim or the evidence you gathered in this investigation help you begin to design and build a lightweight, nonelectric listening device that can enhance a nature walk?

_____

_____

HANDS-ON ACTIVITY

Engineer It
Designing a Listening Device

Design your own hearing-enhancing device to use during an outdoor hike. Your device should not have a battery and should not go in your ear. Be safe—don't put *anything* in your ears.

Form a question What question do you have about the hearing-enhancing device?

Did you know?

Ear trumpets are believed to be the first hearing-enhancing devices. They were first described by Jean Leurechon in 1634.

_____

_____

_____

POSSIBLE MATERIALS

- [ ] plastic cups
- [ ] duct tape
- [ ] scissors
- [ ] paper cups
- [ ] masking tape
- [ ] rubber tubing
- [ ] cloth scraps
- [ ] string

Explore

STEP 1 **Investigate your question** Handle and examine the materials available to you. Brainstorm ideas with your team. Choose the best idea. Then make a rough sketch of how you think your device will look and work.

What are your criteria?

_____

_____

What are your constraints?

_____

_____

STEP 2 **Identify** Choose the materials you will use to construct your device. Write your list in the box below. Explain how the materials you have chosen will help you meet the criteria and constraints.

First Design Notes

LESSON 1 • Engineering Design

Make and Test

STEP 3 With your team, make and test your device. Make sure you don't put anything in your ears.

Improve and Test

STEP 4 Use the test results to improve your device. In the space below, keep a record of the design changes you make. Include a reason for each change. Stop testing and improving when you are satisfied that your device meets the criteria and constraints.

STEP 5 When you are satisfied that the device meets the criteria and constraints, think of a different design that might work even better. If there is time, build and test this second device. You may choose to replan, rebuild, and retest many small improvements, or you may choose to return to an earlier phase.

Make sure that you communicate with others to share information and learn more. At the end of the process, you should have the best solution possible, given the constraints. Your solution is now ready to use and share with others.

Does your design meet the goals of this activity? Support your **claim** with **evidence** and **reasoning.**

_____

_____

Explain why you chose two of your materials.

_____

_____

Draw conclusions If other students looked at your final design, what improvements might they suggest? Why?

_____

_____

Making Sense

How does your work in this investigation help you begin explain how to design and build a lightweight, nonelectric listening device that can enhance a nature walk?

_____

_____

LESSON 1 • Engineering Design   9

EXPLORATION

What is Engineering?
Kitchen Tech

Technology is how humans change the natural world to meet a want or a need. Think about how each technology you see meets a want or a need. What role do engineers play in the technology shown below? Label three technologies in the picture with the letter of the engineering contribution.

a. designed tools to melt and form glass; made a process to cut glass and assemble a frame

b. designed tools to cut, fold, and glue sheets of cardboard into containers

c. designed electric circuits, mechanical parts, and an easy-to-use control panel

Engineering is the process of designing new or improved technology. Engineers are the people who design or improve technology.

Engineers work in many fields, but they often use knowledge from different areas of science to make something new. For example, a mechanical engineer can use knowledge about physics to build things, such as robots. Engineers use critical thinking skills to analyze problems so that they can design possible solutions.

The first part of designing a solution is describing what it must do. What want or need will it address? How will it meet this want or need? Examining how familiar technology is designed and built can help you learn to design a solution, such as a listening device.

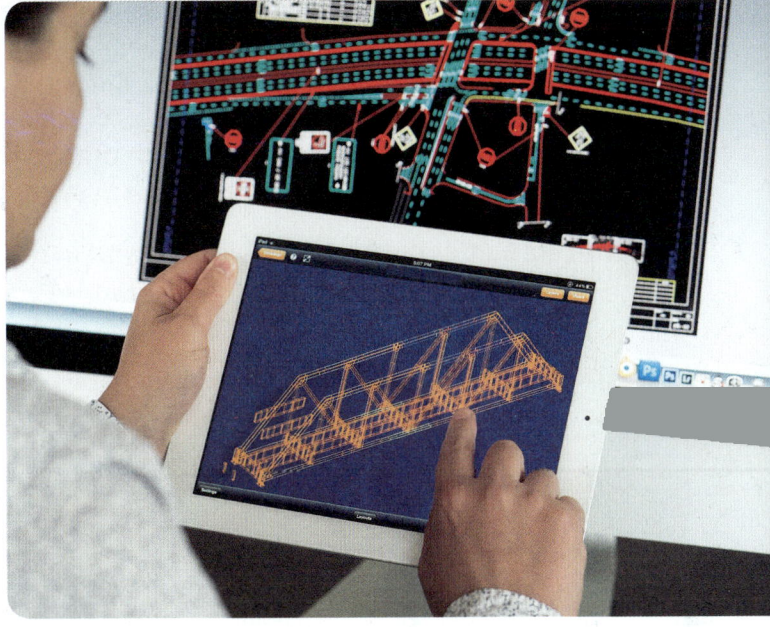

This engineer is at work designing diagrams for an electrical system.

Making Sense

How does the information you learned about engineering help you explain how to build a lightweight, nonelectric listening device that can enhance a nature walk?

_____

_____

_____

Discuss your answer with your group. Provide constructive feedback for each answer and make sure everyone has a chance to speak.

LESSON 1 • Engineering Design

EXPLORATION

How Engineers Solve Problems

Explore

The first step in the engineering design process is the *explore* phase. This phase involves identifying, or defining, a problem.

What are some problems people deal with in the kitchen? View the image of the kitchen in the previous Exploration again. Identify three items in the kitchen that may solve a problem, or meet a want and a need. In the space below, write the name of each item in the left-hand column. Write the need or want the item meets in the right-hand column.

Item	Want or need met

The goal of the explore phase is to learn more about the problem. While exploring the problem you might ask questions, make observations, do research, and identify criteria and constraints.

You learned that when engineers meet a need or a want, they have worked to meet the criteria. For example, people wanted rags that could soak up liquids. Paper towels are considered an improvement on rags because they are more absorbent, and they are disposable.

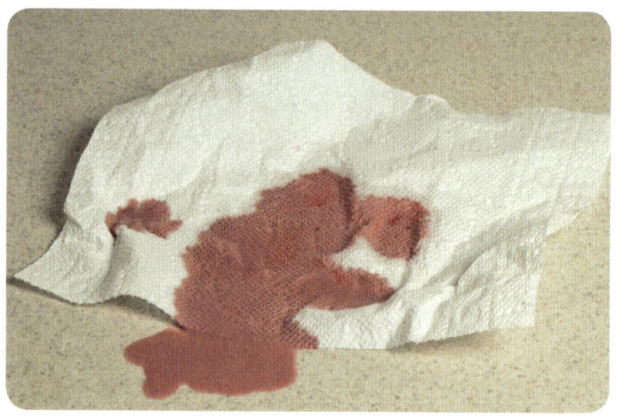

A paper towel is designed to be absorbent and strong so it can soak up liquids without ripping.

LESSON 1 • Engineering Design

Engineers improve solutions all the time. A new solution may not work for everyone, though. Some people may have constraints such as money or space. These constraints affect their decisions about which solutions to buy or use.

Laundry basket

Three-bin laundry basket

Look at the laundry baskets. What constraints might prevent a buyer from choosing the improved three-bin solution?

_____
_____
_____

Once engineers have identified a problem, as well as the criteria and constraints, they have defined the problem. Now engineers are ready to move on to the next phase of the engineering design process.

 Does everyone have to agree on the same constraints? Why or why not? Discuss your answer with your group.

_____
_____
_____

LESSON 1 • Engineering Design

Looking Back to Look Forward

Solutions to problems can have different parts. Looking at other solutions can help engineers improve existing designs. In other words, engineers can learn from past solutions to help them develop new and better solutions.

People have developed many hearing-enhancing devices over time, such as those shown below. Most are not perfect solutions, though. Engineers continue to build on and work to improve solutions.

This early ear trumpet collected and directed sound waves to the listener's ear. The device worked best when sounds were nearby. The small end is held near the ear.

Ear trumpets were later improved with longer tubes that helped amplify sounds. They were easier to hold and direct toward the sound.

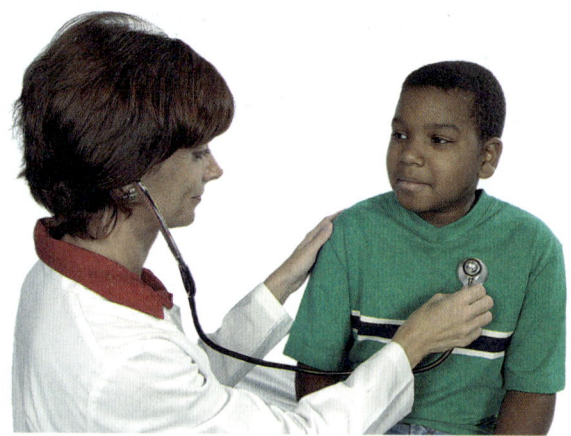

A stethoscope is often used by doctors. Sound travels from the patient to the cup at the end of the stethoscope. This increases the volume of the sound. The sound moves through the tubes to the doctor's ears.

This concrete listening post collects and focuses sounds like a curved mirror. Before radar, the military used posts like this to listen for approaching enemy planes.

Make

Once engineers have defined the problem, they are ready for the *Make and Test* phase. This phase usually involves brainstorming possible solutions for the problem.

When engineers brainstorm, they try to think of as many ideas as possible. Sometimes these ideas may not solve the problem, but that is okay! After they write down a number of ideas, engineers use the criteria, constraints, and the problem statement to narrow down their options and decide which solutions will work best.

Now that engineers have some options, it is time for them to make a plan. A plan likely will be based on one of the ideas from the brainstorming session. In their plans, engineers try to account for how the criteria and constraints will mold and shape their solutions.

Every engineering solution requires following a set of steps.

LESSON 1 • Engineering Design 15

Test

Engineers design many things that people depend on. It's not enough for engineers to say that a design works. They must test and retest the design to ensure it solves the problem. Each design starts out as a **prototype**, or early version, for testing. Prototypes must be thoroughly tested to be sure they're safe and work correctly and consistently.

A **fair test** is one that doesn't give any advantage to the conditions or objects being tested. For a fair test, engineers observe and measure the effects of changing only one thing, or variable, at a time. Changing many variables at once would be quicker. But then testers wouldn't know which variable caused the results. By changing single variables, engineers can determine how to better meet their criteria.

Suppose you want to find the fastest way to walk home. You'll need to time each route as you walk at roughly the same speed on similar days. You can't compare walking the first route, running the second route, and carrying a heavy backpack on the third route. The same is true for the results on a slippery, icy day and on a warm, dry day.

Take a look at the sound-system test room below. Read each caption to find out more about the different parts. Then answer the question on the next page.

a. **Sound source**
A CD, smartphone, TV, or radio is a possible source of test sounds.

b. **Remote control**
A remote control lets testers adjust loudness and choose which speaker to test.

c. **Wall lining**
The wall lining helps keep outside sounds from interfering with sounds in the room.

Your Fair Test

What steps would you take to make a fair test of the speakers shown in the sound-system test room?

_____

_____

Improve and Test

During the *Improve and Test* phase, engineers repeat many of the steps in the *Make and Test* phase. They may replan, rebuild, and retest possible improvements. They may even go back to another idea they brainstormed.

When engineers work on design solutions, team members often communicate with one another. They share their observations to help improve what they are working on and to gain insight on future solutions.

Communication is an important part of most situations. Think of a volleyball team. By talking or sharing signals during practice, players who work as a team will likely play better during a game. An engineering team needs close communication to do its best, too.

Designs can also improve bit by bit as engineers learn more about the materials they're using. Engineers test possible improvements and then add them to the design. The result is the ideal, or best, design possible within the constraints of time, materials, and budget.

After a game, volleyball players may talk about what worked well and what didn't work so well. They also may talk about what they plan to do better during their next practice or game. Likewise, engineers communicate after testing solutions to try to optimize their solutions and designs, or make them as good as possible. Good communication and teamwork help improve any team's final results.

Explain How is communication important to both sports and engineering?

_____

_____

The Engineering Design Process

Here are the steps of the engineering design process you just explored.

In summary, this process has three main parts, or phases, that can be used to solve many different kinds of problems.

Explore

During the *Explore* phase, you learn more about the the problem. Steps you may take include asking questions, doing research, making observations, stating the problem, and identifying the criteria and constrains of the solutions.

Make and Test

During the *Make and Test* phase, you develop solutions. Steps you may take include brainstorming possible solutions, making a plan, making prototypes, testing prototypes, and evaluating possible solutions.

Improve and Test

During the *Improve and Test* phase, you repeat steps from the previous phase. You may replan, rebuild, and retest small improvements, or even go back to an earlier prototype or plan. Throughout this phase, you communicate with your team to share information. By the end of the process, you should have the best possible solution that meets your constraints and criteria.

Making Sense

How does the information you learned about the engineering design process help you begin to explain how to build a lightweight, nonelectric listening device that can enhance a nature walk?

_____

_____

_____

Name _____

Lesson Check

Can You Explain It?

Recall your proposed solution for a listening device. Use what you've learned to do the following:

- Explain the importance of researching previous solutions to the same problem.
- Explain how solutions are designed.
- Describe how and why potential design solutions are tested.

Now I know or think that _____

_____

_____

_____

Making Connections

When the sun is very bright, it can hurt your eyes. What can you do to solve the problem? How is this similar to needing to enhance your hearing?

_____

_____

_____

_____

LESSON 1 • Engineering Design   19

Checkpoints

1. Identify whether each description below is a good or poor design practice. Draw a line from each description to the correct category.

   Good Design Practice

   - have multiple designs
   - skip the testing stage
   - identify criteria and constraints
   - test solutions only once
   - improve multiple times

   Poor Design Practice

2. Circle all the choices that correctly complete this sentence. During the design process, engineers _____.
   a. test solutions to design problems more than once
   b. don't waste time learning about other solutions
   c. don't try to improve others' solutions or their own solutions
   d. create more than one solution to the same problem

3. Janet is trying to improve the design of her lunchbox. Choose the criteria that she should keep in mind.
   a. The lunchbox should be comfortable to carry for long periods.
   b. The lunchbox should keep the food colder.
   c. The lunchbox could use a special pocket for water bottles.
   d. The lunchbox should have sharp corners and rough edges.

4. Karl is conducting an investigation to see if his plants grow better in the window. Construct an explanation to identify the criteria for this to be a fair test.

   _____

   _____

   _____

LESSON 1 • Engineering Design

5. Choose words or phrases from the word bank to complete the sentences about the engineering design process.

| many tries | retest | retesting |
| test | testing | one try |

Engineers _____ designs because it's important to be sure a solution works. Usually _____ happens because it takes _____ to get a working prototype.

6. Use what you've learned in this lesson to plan how to optimize your hearing-enhancing device.

_____
_____
_____
_____

7. The paragraph below summarizes the engineering design process you followed when designing the listening device. Choose words or phrases from the word bank to complete the sentences.

| one part | many parts | no prototypes |
| multiple prototypes | test them only once | retest them many times |

Like real engineers, we are solving a problem. Thus, we should create _____ of our listening devices. The next step is to _____. During our tests, we should change _____ of the design at a time.

Name _____

Unit Review

1. Which two factors define any engineering problem? Circle the correct choice.

   a. making and testing

   b. time and expense

   c. nature and technology

   d. criteria and constraints

2. Examine the structure below. Explain possible criteria that likely influenced the designer who created it.

_____
_____
_____
_____

3. Explain the difference between criteria and constraints. Give an example of each.

_____
_____
_____
_____

22 UNIT 1 • Unit Review

4. You are confronted with the problem of a very dirty dog and decide to use technology to address it. The solution should be the most effective way to clean the dog. Number the steps below from 1 to 8 to show the process you should plan to follow.

_____ Evaluate test results.

_____ Design a prototype.

____1____ Identify the problem.

_____ Retest the modified prototype.

____8____ Construct a final design.

_____ Research existing related technology.

____4____ Build and test the prototype.

_____ Modify the prototype.

5. In addressing the problem above, which steps are you likely to take more than once? Circle all that apply.

a. Evaluate test results.
b. Modify the prototype.
c. Construct a final design.
d. Retest the modified prototype.
e. Identify the problem.

6. Explain why an engineering design solution that does not pass testing can still be considered a success.

_____
_____
_____
_____

7. Which are good reasons for repeated testing in the engineering design processs? Circle all that apply.

    a. to ensure safety

    b. to solve problems

    c. to reduce feedback

    d. to eliminate criteria

    e. to develop a final product

8. Explain the importance of failures in the engineering design process.

_____

_____

_____

_____

9. Develop a plan to find a solution to a problem you would like to solve. Be sure to identify the problem, constraints, and criteria.

_____

_____

_____

_____

_____

10. Engineers are testing a solution to a problem. The solution is failing. What should they do? Select all that apply.

    a. consider using other materials for the design

    b. figure out what didn't go right with the design

    c. decide not to develop other solutions to this problem

    d. understand that sometimes things don't work as planned

In Unit 1, you learned how people's needs led to the development of new technologies. In this unit, you will explore how the needs of living things for surviving and growing can be met by their structures and functions.

UNIT 2 Plant and Animal Structure and Function

Lesson 1
Plant Parts and How They Function 26

Lesson 2
Animal Parts and How They Function 44

Lesson 3
How Senses Work 64

Unit Review 84

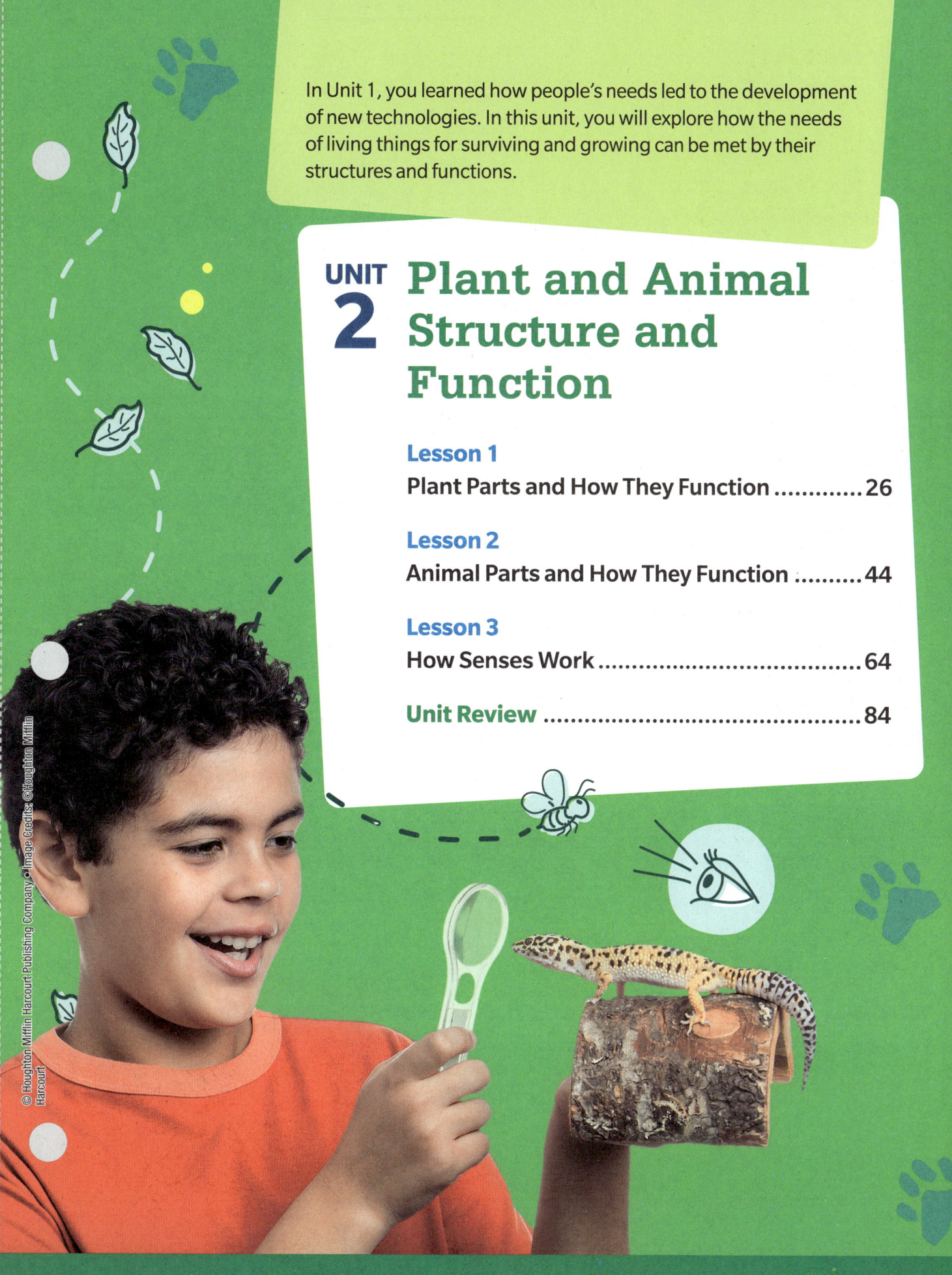

LESSON 1

Plant Parts and How They Function

Does an apple a day *really* keep the doctor away?

What do you notice about the apple tree?

I notice _____

_____

_____

_____

What do you wonder about the apples on the tree?

I wonder _____

_____

_____

_____

Can You Explain It?

Trees are plants that have structures that help them survive, grow, and reproduce. Why do you think some trees produce fruit? Sketch, write, or model your answer.

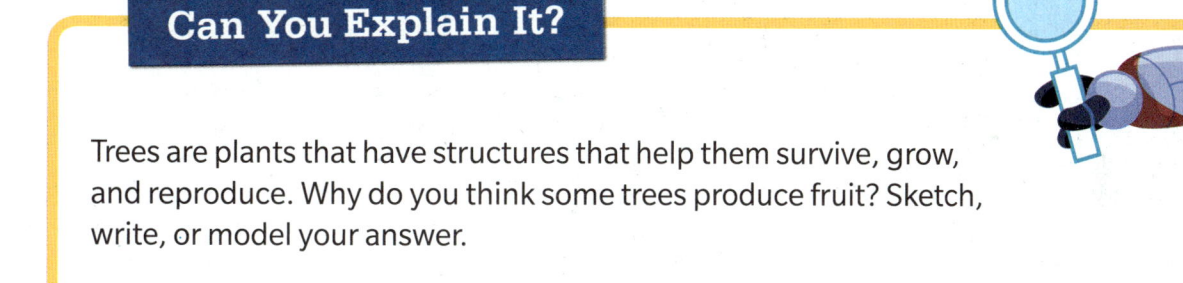

LESSON 1 • Plant Parts and How They Function

HANDS-ON ACTIVITY

Flower Power

The flowers on an apple tree attract bees and other insects. The bees feed on the nectar made by the flowers. When a bee lands on a flower, pollen sticks on its legs and body. The bee flies from one tree to another, and pollen falls off into other flowers. The trees need this pollen to make new fruit. The process is called *pollination*. Pollination occurs as the result of the bee, flower and pollen working as a system.

Form a question Ask a question about the different parts that make up a flower.

_____

_____

Did you know?
It takes an apple tree four to five years to produce its first fruit.

LESSON 1 • Plant Parts and How They Function

Parts of a Flower

The diagram of a flower below shows the parts of a flower. These parts work together as a system to ensure the plant can reproduce. Explore each part to understand their function.

The **anther** is part of the stamen. This male structure sits on top of a long **filament** and produces pollen. When pollen comes into contact with an ovule, a seed is produced.

The **stamen** is a male part of a flower that contains the anther and filament.

The **pistil** is a female part of the flower. Its enlarged base is called the ovary.

The **ovule**, also called an *egg*, is inside the **ovary**. It is a female structure. If pollen reaches an ovule, a seed is produced.

The **sepals** are the outer parts of a flower that cover the flower bud. They protect the flower while it is developing.

The **petals** make up the outside of a flower. Petals are often brightly colored and scented to attract insects and birds that pollinate the plants.

Describe Choose the correct words from the diagram that complete the sentences below.

The _____ are plant parts that cover and protect the flower bud. The function of the _____ is to make pollen. If pollen comes into contact with an _____, a seed is produced.

POSSIBLE MATERIALS

- [ ] flower on a stem
- [ ] scissors
- [ ] gloves
- [ ] newspaper
- [ ] tweezers
- [ ] hand lens

STEP 1 **Investigate your question** The sepal, petal, stamen (including the anther) and pistil (including the ovule) create a system. Identify those parts on your flower.

STEP 2 **Organize your data** Use this space below to draw a model of your flower. Include all of the parts you've identified.

30 LESSON 1 • Plant Parts and How They Function

Communicate Share your model with other groups. Explain differences or similarities among the group's model.

_____
_____
_____
_____

Draw conclusions Make a **claim** about how the parts of a flower create a system. Support your claim with **evidence** from your investigation and explain your **reasoning**.

_____
_____
_____
_____

Making Sense

How does your claim or the evidence you gathered in this investigation help you begin to explain why trees produce fruit?

_____
_____
_____

HANDS-ON ACTIVITY

Slurp!

The roots of a plant take in water and minerals from soil. How does the plant use the water? A plant needs water and nutrients, such as minerals, to grow and reproduce. In this investigation, you will explore how water is transported through a plant stem system.

Form a question Ask a question about how water and nutrients travel through a plant.

Did you know?

The shepherd's tree, which grows in South Africa, has roots that reach down 68 meters. That's six times its height!

LESSON 1 • Plant Parts and How They Function

POSSIBLE MATERIALS

- [ ] clear plastic cup
- [ ] water
- [ ] food coloring
- [ ] celery
- [ ] plastic knife
- [ ] newspaper

STEP 1 **Investigate your question** In the space below, plan a fair test that will help you gather evidence to explain how plants transport water. List the materials you will use. You may choose to write or draw the steps. After getting your teacher's approval, carry out your investigation.

LESSON 1 • Plant Parts and How They Function

Make observations Describe the appearance of the celery before and after your investigation.

_____
_____
_____

In the space below, list one example of good communication and teamwork that you followed during this investigation.

_____
_____

Draw conclusions Make a **claim** about the movement of water in plants. Use **evidence** to support your claim. Explain your **reasoning**.

_____
_____

Make a model Using what you can infer about the way water moves in celery, make a 3D model of a plant's water system. Your model does not need to function, but you should use different materials to represent the different parts of the plant.

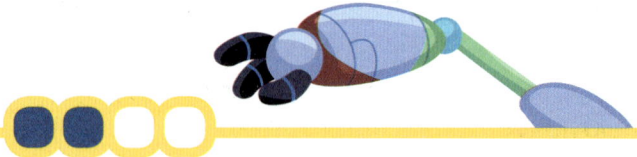

Making Sense

How does understanding how water and nutrients move through a plant's systems help you understand how and why trees grow fruit?

_____
_____
_____

LESSON 1 • Plant Parts and How They Function

EXPLORATION

Plant Structures Have Special Functions

What Do Plant Parts Do?

You can tell from a quick glance at a plant that it has different structures. **Structures** are the physical parts of living things. Many plants have similar structures that perform similar functions. Together these parts create a system to help the plant survive. A system is something with parts that work together.

Plants have two main systems: roots and shoots. Roots grow below ground. Shoots, which include leaves, stems, buds, flowers, and fruit, typically grow above ground.

Leaves capture sunlight and use it to make food in the form of sugar. Plants use the sugar to grow.

Stems support leaves and help plants stay upright.

Roots help hold a plant in place. They also absorb water and nutrients from the soil. Plants need the water and nutrients to grow and reproduce.

LESSON 1 • Plant Parts and How They Function

Similar but Different

When you look around at different plants, you see that they often have similar structures—roots, stems, leaves, flowers, and more. But these structures do not look exactly the same in all plants. Leaves and flowers differ in shape, size, and color. Some plants have thorns. Others do not.

Compare the functions of the plant structures in each set of photos. Write whether the parts most support *protection*, *growth*, or *reproduction*.

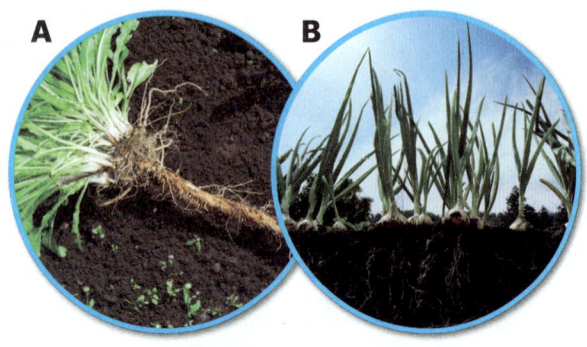

A. A **taproot** can get water from deep underground, and it does well in droughts. It can also store sugar.

B. **Fibrous roots** can quickly absorb water and nutrients near the soil's surface. They also help stop soil erosion.

C. Large, flat **leaves** capture sunlight. Having lots of large leaves in spring and summer allows plants to absorb more sunlight and make more food.

D. The **needles** of evergreens, such as pine trees, gather sunlight for the plant to make food. The needles' shape and waxy coating reduce water loss in dry weather.

E. **Woody stems** help plants such as trees and shrubs stay upright in strong winds. These stems can help trees become very tall. Tall plants get more sunlight.

F. Other plants, such as dandelions and sunflowers, have **green stems.** These stems can capture sunlight while they hold the plants up and support branches, leaves, and other parts.

36 **LESSON 1** • Plant Parts and How They Function

G. Plants such as dandelions and apple trees produce **flowers**. A flower has different parts that are involved in reproduction, including petals and the pollen-producing stamen. Many flowers attract animals that move pollen from one plant to another. In some plants, such as apple trees, flowers develop into fruit. Fruit contains and protects seeds.

H. Plants such as pine trees make **cones** instead of flowers. Male cones release pollen that pollinates female cones. Female cones then hold seeds until they are ready to be released. New plants grow from seeds that land in places with the right conditions.

I. Other types of plants, such as ferns, reproduce using **spores**. When spores are released, they are carried by wind. If spores land in a place with the right conditions, new plants will grow.

J. Some plants, such as roses, have **thorns** with sharp, pointed ends that can injure an animal that tries to eat the plant.

K. Tough, thick **bark** prevents many animals from eating trees and shrubs. It also helps prevent fungi or bacteria from getting into a plant and causing disease.

L. Cacti and other plants that live in dry areas have leaves shaped like **spines**. An animal that tries to eat a spiny plant will likely be injured.

LESSON 1 • Plant Parts and How They Function

It's What's Inside That Counts

A plant's root system absorbs water and minerals from soil. A plant's shoot system has other structures to help get the water and minerals to its other parts.

Take a closer look at the inside of the stems in the two plants below. Each one has a different system of tubes that helps the plant survive and grow.

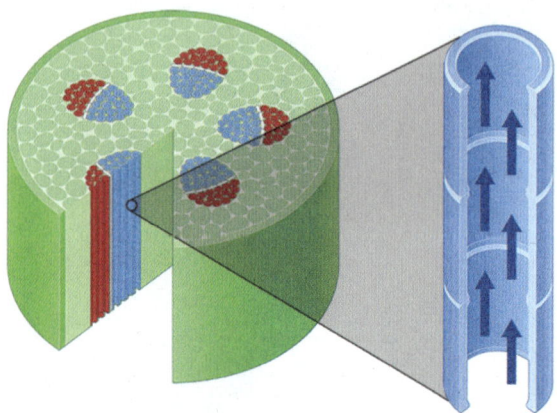
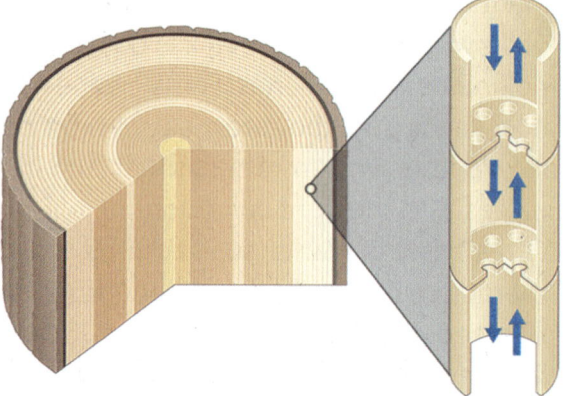

Inside a plant stem is a system of **water-carrying tubes.** Water is taken in from the roots. The water moves up from the roots through the tubes into the plant's leaves. The leaves can then use the water to make food.

Sugar made in a plant's leaves moves through a system of **food-carrying tubes.** These tubes travel from the leaves through the plant, all the way down to the roots. Some plant roots, such as carrots, store extra sugar made by the plant.

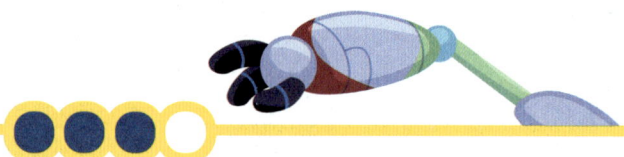

Making Sense

Describe the plant systems evidence you have that supports your claim about why trees make fruit. What is the function of fruit?

EXPLORATION

How Plants Change

Seasonal Changes

In nature, many plants live in environments where conditions change throughout the year. Seasonal changes can be especially difficult. Whatever the conditions, plants need to absorb sunlight, make food, grow, survive, and reproduce. How do the ways plants change seasonally help them to survive changing conditions?

winter

summer

spring

autumn

In the picture of autumn, the leaves are changing color and beginning to fall to the ground. What factors might affect when a tree begins to lose its leaves?

_____

_____

For plants, the major indicator of seasonal change is the change in the amount of light. For example, northern regions have fewer hours of daylight in the winter than they do in the summer. Plants respond to changes in the lengths of day and night. Special structures in plants' leaves detect these changes. When certain seasonal conditions are met, plants can begin budding, forming flowers, or dropping their leaves.

How Do You Grow?

Read about plant behaviors, and then complete the activity.

Plants **respond to light.** Plants need sunlight to make food, so a house plant that sits in front of a window will grow toward the light. If the plant is not turned regularly, it will become very lopsided. Circle the image (a or b) that shows what will happen if this plant is not turned at the window.

The roots of plants grow down toward the center of Earth in **response to gravity.** The stem of a plant grows in the opposite direction, away from the center of Earth. This usually results in the stem growing upward. Circle the image (a or b) that shows how the stem and roots will respond if this plant is knocked over.

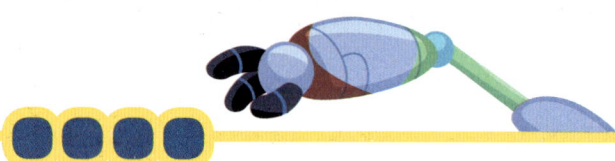

Making Sense

Describe the evidence you have found to support your claim about why trees make fruit. Why is fruit produced only during certain times of the year?

_____

_____

_____

Name _____

Lesson Check

Can You Explain It?

Review your ideas from the beginning of this lesson about why some trees grow fruit. How have your ideas changed? Be sure to do the following:

- Define the term *structure*.
- Explain how seasonal changes affect plants.
- Use data from investigations and explorations to explain the different functions of plant structures and how they work together as a system.

Now I know or think that _____

_____

_____

_____

Making Connections

Not all fruits grow on trees. How might the structures of a plant that grows low to the ground compare to the structures found on a tree?

_____

_____

_____

_____

LESSON 1 • **Plant Parts and How They Function**

Checkpoints

1. Study the images. On each image, write the letter that corresponds to the material carried by the system of tubes marked by arrows. All labels may not apply.

   a. food
   b. soil
   c. water
   d. heat

2. Read the claim: Roots are involved in plant growth. Which evidence supports this claim?

   a. Roots absorb water, which plants need to make food.
   b. Roots capture sunlight, which gives plants a source of energy for making food.
   c. Roots help protect plants from animals.
   d. Roots are involved in plant reproduction.

3. Which answer correctly states how a plant's food system functions?

   a. Leaves absorb water, which plants need to make food.
   b. Leaves produce food using sunlight, and food moves around the tubes to the rest of the plant.
   c. Roots absorb nutrients, and nutrients move up the tubes and turn to sugar.

4. Plants have systems that allow them to respond to their environments. Use the terms to complete the sentences.

   Plants respond to _____ when they bend toward windows. In response to _____, plant parts bend up or down so that each part is in the right position to do its job.

   gravity
   light

5. Which of these plant parts are most involved in protecting it from animals? Circle all that apply.

   a. bark

   b. leaves

   c. spines

   d. thorns

6. Use the terms to identify the function of each structure.

> growth   reproduction   protection

stem

roots

flowers

spines

7. How are thorns on a rose similar to spines on a cactus? Use evidence to support your answer.

_____

_____

_____

8. Support this claim using evidence: Roots are part of a system that allow plants to grow.

_____

_____

LESSON 2

Animal Parts and How They Function

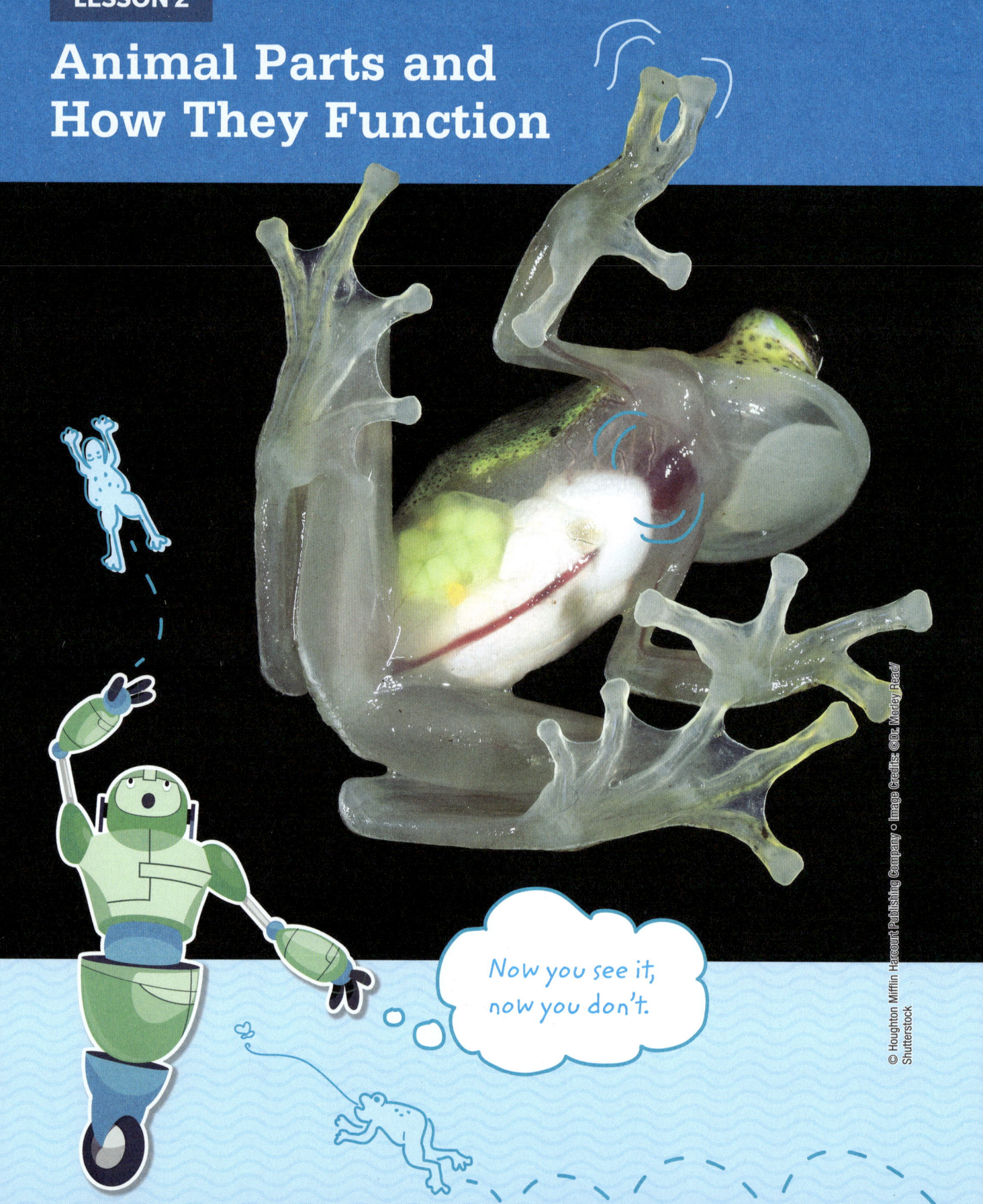

Now you see it, now you don't.

What do you notice about the glass frog?

I notice _____
_____
_____

What do you wonder about the structures that you can see on the outside and the inside of the glass frog?

I wonder _____
_____
_____
_____

Can You Explain It?

What structures and behaviors do you think help a glass frog live, survive, and reproduce in the tropical rain forest? Sketch, write, or model your answer.

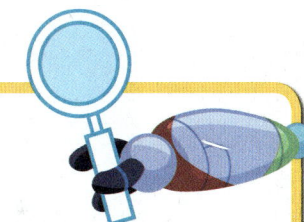

LESSON 2 • Animal Parts and How They Function

HANDS-ON ACTIVITY

Dinner is Served

Different kinds of animals eat different kinds of food. Some animals feed on plants. Hummingbirds have long, thin beaks and tongues that help them feed on flower nectar. Some animals eat other animals. Glass frogs eat insects, which they catch in their wide-open mouths.

Form a question Ask a question about the structures an animal uses to eat food.

_____
_____
_____
_____

Did you know?

A hummingbird must eat about half its body weight in sugar every day to stay alive.

Time to Eat!

Mountain lions have powerful jaws and very sharp teeth.

Antelope have mouths with flat teeth at the front. This allows them to bite grass that grows close to the ground.

Giant tubeworms have no mouths! Tubeworms get nutrients from tiny organisms that live inside them.

Eagles have very large, hooked beaks that easily tear apart flesh.

Frogs have flexible jaws they can open wide to snatch food with their long, sticky tongues.

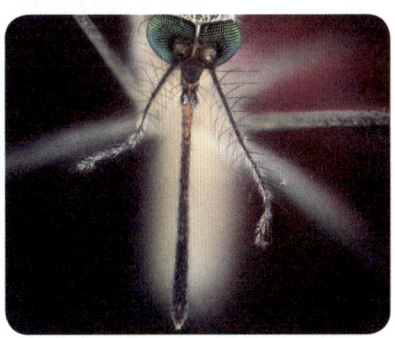
Female mosquitoes use their tubelike mouth parts to pierce skin and suck blood.

Classify What do these animals eat based on the structures of their mouth parts? What inferences can you make?

Animal	What does it eat?	What's your evidence?
mountain lion		
antelope		
female mosquito		
eagle		
frog		
giant tubeworm		

LESSON 2 • Animal Parts and How They Function

POSSIBLE MATERIALS
- [ ] plastic spoons
- [ ] paper clips
- [ ] paper
- [ ] chopsticks
- [ ] marbles
- [ ] cup
- [ ] tweezers

STEP 1 **Investigate your question** In the space below, plan a fair test to investigate external structures that help animals eat. List the materials you will use. You may choose to write or draw the steps.

STEP 2 Carry out your plan, and record your results. Present your data in a way that allows everyone to see what you did and what happened. You might present your information in a table or a graph. Or you might choose to design a poster with photographs and text.

Draw conclusions Make a **claim** that answers the question you decided to explore. Support your claim with **evidence** from your investigation and **reasoning** to explain how the evidence supports your claim.

_____
_____
_____
_____

Making Sense

How does your claim or the evidence you gathered in this investigation help you begin to explain how a glass frog's structures help it survive?

_____
_____
_____
_____

LESSON 2 • Animal Parts and How They Function

HANDS-ON ACTIVITY

Courtship Displays

Reproduction usually requires a male and a female. So how does an animal choose a mate? Some animals, such as frogs and birds, have special calls or songs that attract mates. Other animals put on a show! The male of a species often performs special behaviors to attract a female. The female can use this behavior to judge how strong and healthy her potential mate is.

For example, a male peacock spider does a special dance. A male quetzal shows his brightly-colored tail feathers. These behaviors, called courtship displays, increase these animals' chances to reproduce.

Form a question Ask a question about how animals use internal and external structures to attract mates.

Did you know?

A peacock spider is barely larger than a grain of rice. Special cameras are used to photograph them.

Research Work with a partner. Research other animals that use internal and external structures along with special behaviors to find a mate. Choose two animals. Then make a multimedia presentation about their courtship displays for your class. Remember to use pictures and videos to make your presentation more interesting.

Draw conclusions Make a **claim** that answers the question you decided to explore. Support your claim with **evidence** from your investigation and use **reasoning** to explain how the evidence supports your claim.

_____
_____
_____
_____

 In the space below, list two examples of good communication and teamwork that you followed during this investigation.

_____
_____

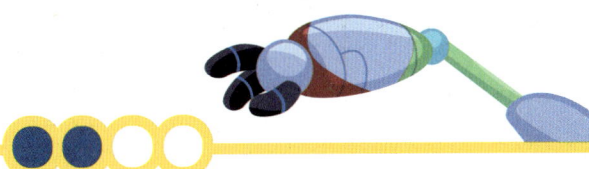

Making Sense

How do animals use internal and external structures along with courtship displays to increase their reproduction chances?

_____
_____
_____
_____

LESSON 2 • Animal Parts and How They Function

EXPLORATION

Body Building

Animals that live in different environments have to deal with different conditions. These conditions affect the body structures of the animals that live in those environments.

Animals have external structures that work together as a system to support survival, growth, behavior, and reproduction. External structures are structures on the outside of an organism.

Take Cover

Animals can be soft, hard, rough, slimy, or spiny. These different kinds of coverings protect the inside of an animal's body.

Moisture and air pass easily through the thin, moist skin of a frog. The skin also makes a slimy substance that keeps it from drying out in warm environments, such as tropical rain forests.

Polar bears have thick hairs that trap heat produced by their bodies. This keeps them warm in the cold Arctic. The transparent, hollow hairs appear white, allowing polar bears to blend into their environment.

Fur insulates this alpaca, preventing heat loss in the cold mountains.

Birds have feathers to keep warm. Birds also need feathers to help them fly.

Some animals, such as porcupines, have sharp spines on their skin to keep them safe.

A sea cucumber's leathery skin protects it from some predators.

A hard shell covers some animals, such as tortoises, for protection.

A snake's scales help it move by gripping and pushing against surfaces.

LESSON 2 • Animal Parts and How They Function 53

Moving Parts

Animals have structures that help them move. These external structures include legs, wings, and fins.

Ants crawl along on three pairs of legs, allowing them to move quickly for their size.

Frogs have two strong hind legs that help them jump high and far.

Bat wings are thin, stretchy membranes made of skin that catch the air to fly.

Pigeons flap their feathered wings to move through the air.

Sharks swing their tails from side to side in the water to help them glide forward.

Dolphins push their tails up and down to move forward in the water.

Moving Through the Environment

Animals are *adapted* to, or fit well in, the environments in which they live. They have external body parts that allow them to move about on land, in the air, or through the water.

LAND, AIR, OR WATER?

Choose one of the animals below. Construct an argument as to whether the animal best moves on land, in air or in water. Support your argument with evidence describing what structures aide in their movement.

_____

_____

_____

 Discuss your answers with your group. Provide constructive feedback for each answer and make sure everyone has a chance to speak.

Although most animals have structures for moving in their environment, some animals don't often move from place to place. Corals, sponges, and barnacles are animals that mostly stay in one spot. These animals have structures that help them catch food since they can't move around to find it.

LESSON 2 • Animal Parts and How They Function

How Animals Reproduce

You have learned that plants have special structures for reproduction. Animals have reproductive structures, too. Some of these structures are internal, or on the inside, of animals. Some are external, or on the outside, of animals. Different animals reproduce in different ways.

Female birds have internal structures to grow and lay eggs. A male bird fertilizes the eggs while they are in the female bird. Young then develop in the eggs outside the female bird's body. Most adult birds care for their young until they are old enough to leave the nest.

A female fish also has an internal structure that helps her form and lay eggs. In many species, a male fish fertilizes the eggs after they are laid. Most fish produce many eggs, and they do not take care of their young. Amphibians, such as frogs, use a similar method to reproduce.

Many reptiles lay eggs. Others have structures that allow young to grow inside their bodies. Some reptiles take care of their young, and some do not. Turtles do not typically protect their eggs or take care of their young.

Most insect species lay eggs and do not take care of their young. Others, such as ants and bees, care for their developing young, which are called larvae. In an ant colony, worker ants provide food to larvae to help them grow.

An adult mollusk, such as a clam or oyster, releases eggs into the water. Eggs that are fertilized eventually grow into young mollusks.

Mammals, such as deer, have structures that allow their young to develop inside their bodies. When the animal is born, its parents feed it and care for it until it is bigger, stronger, and can find its own food.

Comparing Reproduction Methods

Choose the correct word or phrase to complete each sentence.

| larvae | live young | reproduction | fertilizes |
| external structures | internal structures | pollination | eggs |

When animals make a new animal, _____ occurs. Animals reproduce in different ways. After a female fish lays eggs, a male fish then _____ the eggs. Fish usually do not take care of their young. Other animals, such as mammals, have _____ that allow offspring to grow inside their bodies. They give birth to _____ and care for them after they are born.

Making Sense

Describe the evidence you have found to support your claim about how a glass frog's external structures work together as a system to help it grow, survive and reproduce.

LESSON 2 • Animal Parts and How They Function

EXPLORATION

Inside Out

You have learned about animals' external structures. They also have *internal structures* that support their growth and survival. Internal structures are structures on the inside of an organism. Look at some of this dog's internal structures.

Do you recognize some that you have, too?

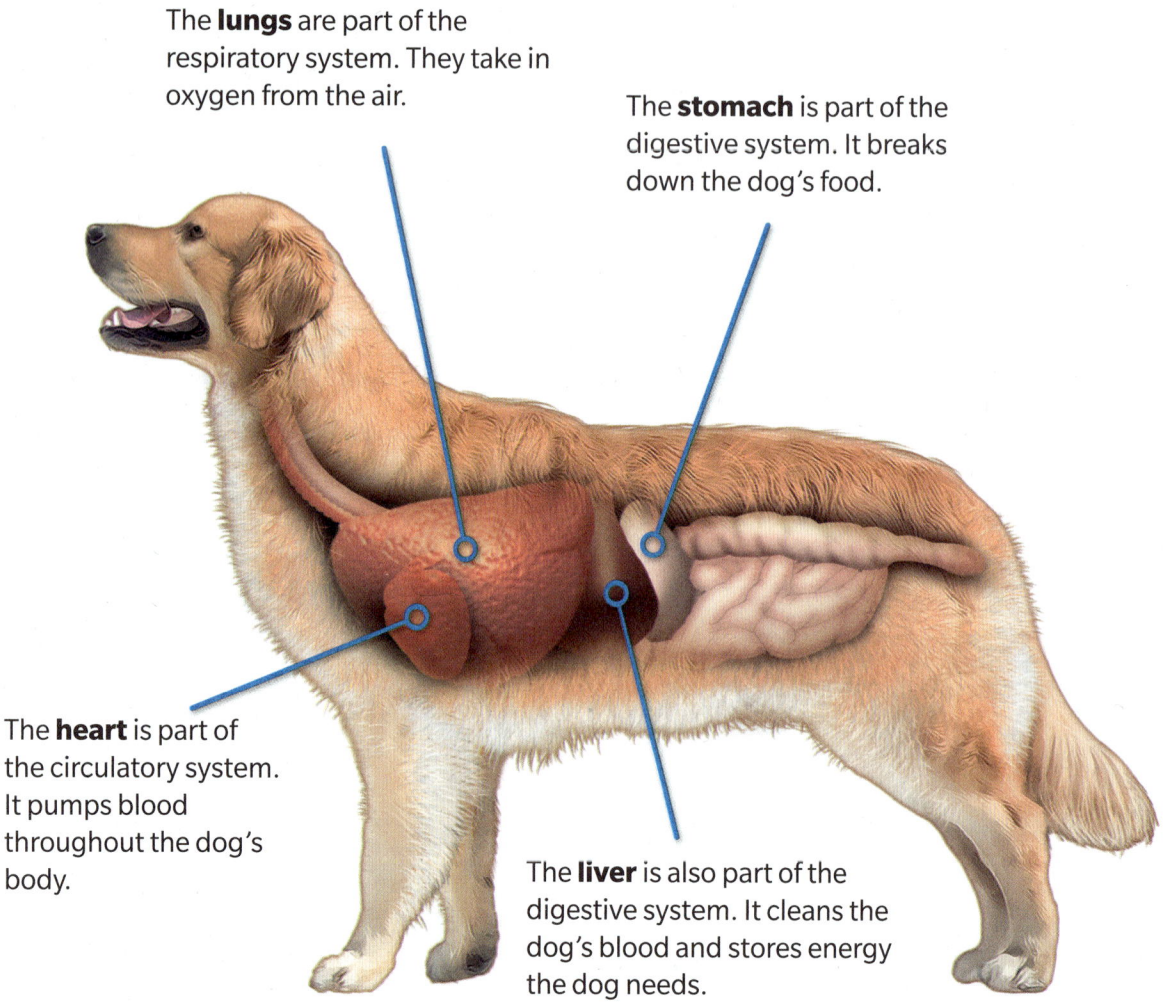

The **lungs** are part of the respiratory system. They take in oxygen from the air.

The **stomach** is part of the digestive system. It breaks down the dog's food.

The **heart** is part of the circulatory system. It pumps blood throughout the dog's body.

The **liver** is also part of the digestive system. It cleans the dog's blood and stores energy the dog needs.

A system is something with parts that work together. Humans and other animals have body systems. The circulatory system includes the heart, blood, veins, and arteries. The respiratory system includes the lungs, nose, and mouth. All the body's systems—and structures within those systems—work together in different ways to help an animal grow, survive, and reproduce. For example, the heart in the circulatory system and the lungs in the respiratory system work together to move blood and oxygen throughout a dog's body.

Get In My Belly!

The digestive system breaks down the foods animals eat into nutrients that their bodies absorb and use.

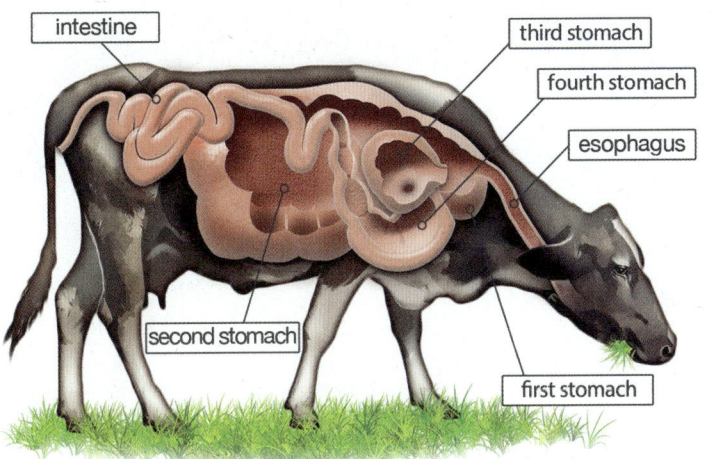

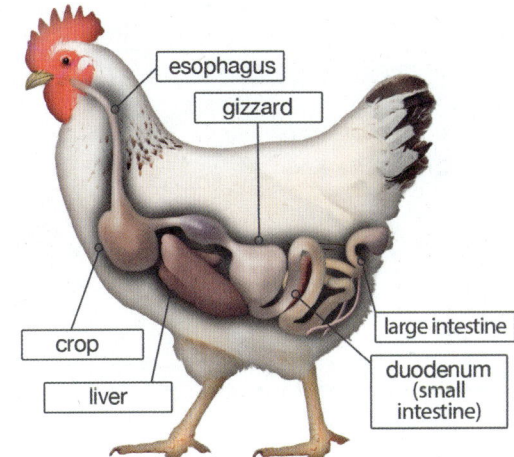

Cows have a stomach with four parts. A cow needs to chew and swallow its food several times during digestion.

Chickens have a gizzard, which is like a stomach. Chickens and some other birds also have a crop, which holds food until it can be sent to the digestive system.

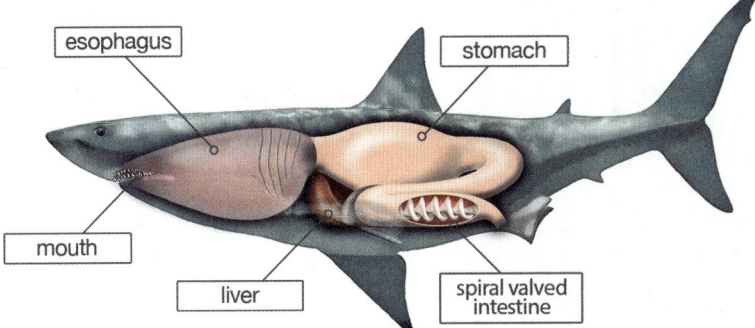

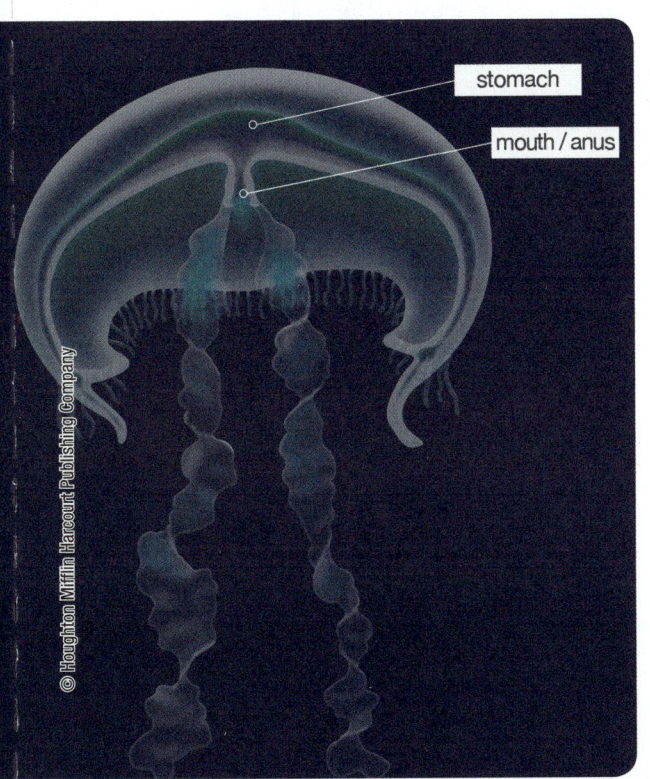

Sharks have spiral-shaped intestines and a *U*-shaped stomach to break down food that they sometimes swallow whole!

Jellyfish do not have digestive systems. Food enters the mouth and is broken down in the body. Waste then leaves through the same opening.

LESSON 2 • Animal Parts and How They Function

Heart to Heart

The circulatory system transports blood around an animal's body.

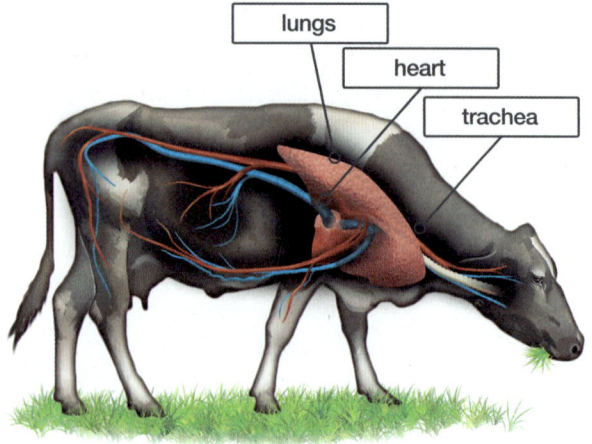

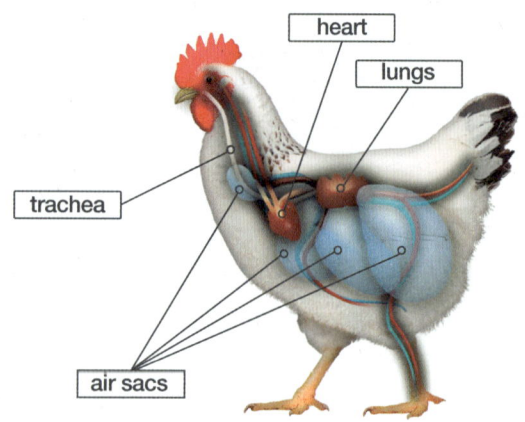

A cow's heart pumps blood through arteries to the cow's different body parts. Veins carry blood back to the heart and then to the lungs.

Birds, such as this chicken, have large hearts. A bird's heart helps keep its body at the right temperature.

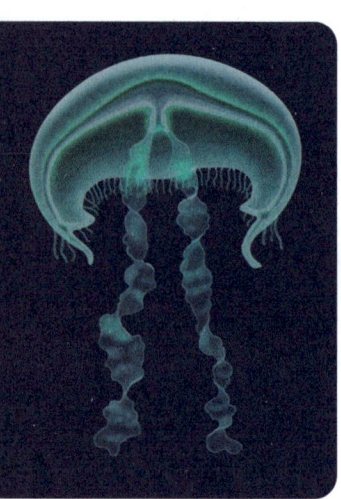

Jellyfish do not have a circulatory system. They don't have a respiratory system, either. They exchange gases through their skin.

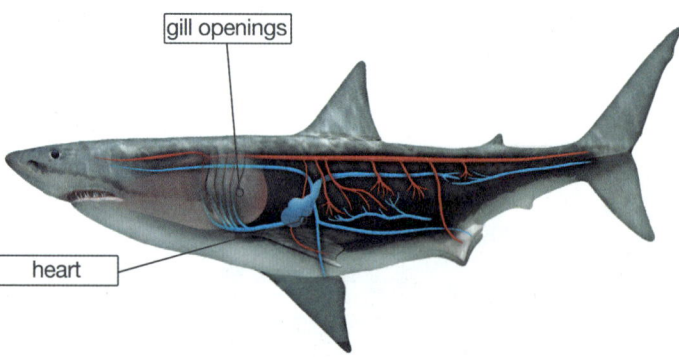

A shark's heart has two chambers and is shaped like the letter S. Sharks do not have lungs. They have gills instead.

Making Sense

How does your understanding of how internal structures work together as a system help you to explain how a glass frog survives in the tropical rain forest?

Name _____

Lesson Check

Can You Explain It?

Review your ideas from the beginning of this lesson about what animals need to survive and grow. How have your ideas changed? Be sure to do the following:

- Identify the functions of a glass frog's internal and external body parts.
- Use data you gathered to explain how the glass frog's body systems help it to survive in the tropical rain forest.

Now I know or think that _____

_____

_____

_____

Making Connections

A parrotfish lives underwater. A glass frog lives in trees high in the tropical rain forest. How might the body structures and functions of a fish be different from those of a frog? How are they the same?

_____

_____

_____

_____

_____

LESSON 2 • Animal Parts and How They Function   61

Checkpoints

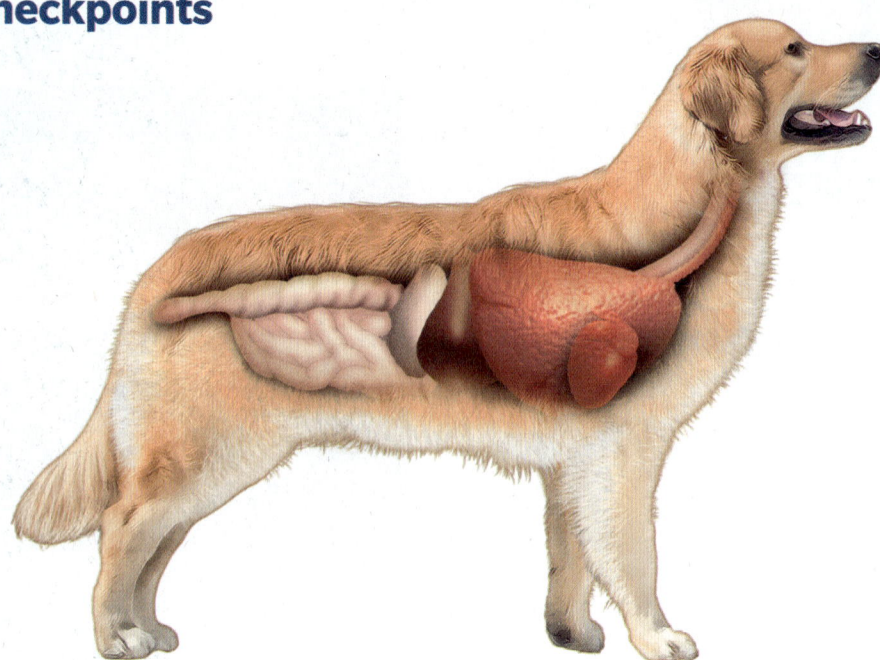

1. Look at the image of the dog. Write the name of each internal structure in the correct column.

   > heart   lungs   stomach   arteries   intestines   liver   veins

Circulatory system	Digestive system

2. Draw a model of a structure or system that functions to protect an animal from predators.

3. Draw lines to connect the components of systems to the functions they perform.

a seagull's wings		a tiger's padded feet
	eating	
a snake's fangs		a frog's tongue
	movement	
an ant's mouth parts		an ostrich's long legs

4. Choose the word or phrase that completes each sentence below.

| fertilized ovule | pollinated female | care for larvae | male adults |

Like plants, most animals need both

_____ and _____

structures to reproduce. Queen ants lay

_____ eggs in a nest.

5. Label the parts of the shark that are involved in the digestive system in this model.

   a. esophagus
   b. liver
   c. intestines
   d. stomach

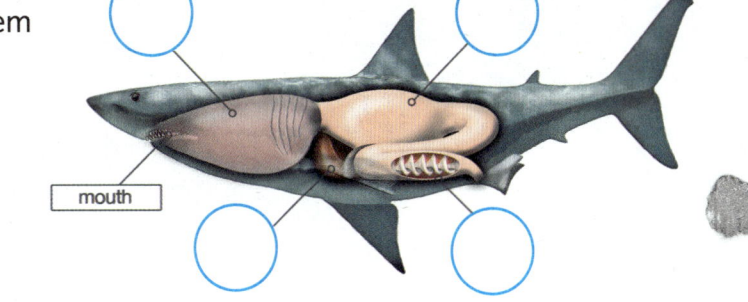

mouth

6. Referring to the model of the shark above, use evidence to construct an argument about what would happen if the shark were missing any part of its digestive system.

_____

_____

_____

_____

LESSON 2 • Animal Parts and How They Function

LESSON 3
How Senses Work

Time to eat!

What do you notice about the bat and the plant?

I notice _____

_____

_____

_____

What do you wonder about the conditions in which the bat is feeding?

I wonder _____

_____

_____

_____

Can You Explain It?

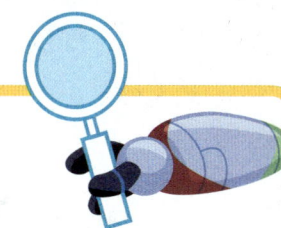

How does a bat use its senses to find food? Sketch, write, or model your answer.

LESSON 3 • How Senses Work   65

HANDS-ON ACTIVITY

Touch Test

Bats have tiny hairs on their wings that let them sense the speed and direction of air over their wings. These hairs help bats know when they should fly faster or slower. This allows bats to move skillfully through the air and avoid stalling during flight.

Your skin has sensory structures, too. The sensory structures in your skin are not arranged evenly across your body. Some parts of your body may have more of one kind of structure but fewer of another.

Form a question Ask a question about how your skin detects touch and pressure.

_____

_____

Did you know?

The largest fruit bats have a wingspan of up to 2 meters (6 feet) from tip to tip!

POSSIBLE MATERIALS
- [ ] 2 paper clips
- [ ] metric ruler
- [ ] pencil or pen

Procedure

STEP 1 Open and bend the paper clips into a V-shape so that each paper clip's ends are about 2 cm apart. Use a metric ruler to measure the distance. Make sure the two halves of the V-shape are the same length.

STEP 2 Ask your partner to rest his or her hand, palm side down, on a flat surface. Tell your partner to look away.

STEP 3 Lightly press both ends of one paper clip into the back of your partner's hand. Do not press too hard! Make sure both ends touch the skin at the same time.

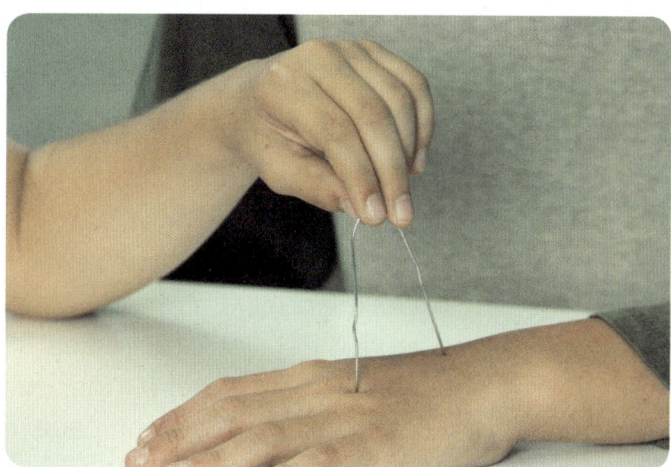

Why do you not want to press down too hard with the paper clip?

LESSON 3 • How Senses Work

STEP 4 Ask your partner if he or she feels one or two pressure points. If your partner feels one point, spread the ends of the paper clip farther apart and test again. If your partner feels two points, push the ends a little closer together and try again. When your partner FIRST feels two points, record the distance between the paper clip's ends.

Think back to Step 1, when you made sure both halves of the V-shaped clip were the same length. Why is that important?

_____

_____

STEP 5 Repeat steps 3 and 4 two more times. Record your results for all three trials by writing the smallest distance at which your partner reports feeling two points.

STEP 6 Repeat steps 3 to 5 on the right shoulder, the right calf, and the inside of the right forearm. You can use another data table and repeat the procedure with your partner doing the testing using the second paper clip.

Body part	Distance		
	Trial 1	Trial 2	Trial 3
Hand			
Shoulder			
Calf			
Forearm			

What was the shortest distance you recorded on your data table?

What was the greatest distance?

_____

On what part of the body were the two points of the paper clip felt at the shortest distance?

_____

On what part of the body were the two points felt at the greatest distance?

_____

On what part of the body did it take the most tries to feel the two distinct points of the paper clip?

_____
_____
_____
_____

How did your results compare to your partner's results?

_____
_____
_____
_____

Draw conclusions Based on your results, make a **claim** about which of the four body parts tested has the most touch sense structures. Support your answer with **evidence** and **reasoning.**

_____
_____
_____

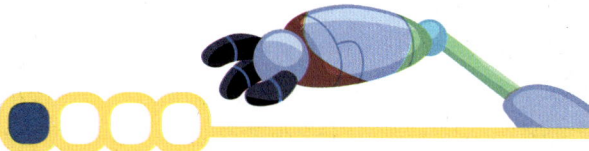

Making Sense

How does your claim or the evidence you gathered in this investigation help you begin to explain how bats might use their senses to find food?

_____
_____

HANDS-ON ACTIVITY

No Smell, No Taste, No See

Your body has structures that help you identify food. Oftentimes, you first use your eyes to tell whether food is ready or safe to eat, such as when fruit is ripe or something looks like it is going bad. You also can use your nose to identify some of these things.

Every time you breathe air into your nose, structures inside it sense different chemicals in the air. These smell structures send signals to the brain about those chemicals. This is how you are able to smell odors and aromas in the air.

Surprisingly, much of your ability to taste comes from your ability to smell. Taste buds on your tongue react to salty, sour, sweet, savory, and bitter flavors. However, it's your ability to smell that allows you to specifically identify a particular food.

Form a question What question do you have about your abilities to see, smell, and taste?

_____

_____

Did you know?

Elephants have 1,948 smell receptors. Humans only have 396.

LESSON 3 • How Senses Work

POSSIBLE MATERIALS

- [ ] blindfold
- [ ] tape
- [ ] cardboard
- [ ] various scented items
- [ ] shoe box
- [ ] construction paper
- [ ] various food items
- [ ] scissors

STEP 1 Try a simple activity to test your ability to smell. Blindfold your partner and see how many smells he or she can identify correctly. Hold a scented item in front of your partner's nose. Keep track of your results. Switch with your partner and repeat.

Did your results surprise you? Why or why not? Which scents did you guess correctly?

_____

_____

_____

STEP 2 Blindfold a partner. Have your partner hold his or her nose. Then, give him or her four different foods to eat. Ask your partner to identify each food. Switch with your partner and repeat, using four different foods. Make sure to wash your hands before handling the food.

What are your results? How do you think your daily life would change if you could not smell?

_____

_____

_____

LESSON 3 • How Senses Work 71

STEP 3 Next, build your vision box. Cut or poke five holes in the top of the box your teacher provides. Cut or poke one small hole on the short side of the box. Then, cut out five flaps of construction paper and cardboard that will each cover one hole on the top of the box. Arrange each paper flap over each hole. Tape one side of the paper to the box so that you end up with five flaps. Repeat this step with the cardboard, making sure to tape the cardboard flap on the same side as the construction paper flap.

STEP 4 Place an item in the box while your partner is looking away. Use your fingers to hold the cardboard flaps shut. Then, have your partner look through the eye hole on the side of the box. Have your partner try to identify the item. If he or she cannot identify the item, open one of the flaps. Continue to open the flaps until your partner can identify the item.

STEP 5 Repeat Step 4, but switch roles with your partner.

What was your object? How many flaps had to be opened for you to identify the object?

_____

_____

What was your partner's object? How many flaps did you have to open for your partner to identify the object?

_____

_____

What did it look like in the box before you started opening the flaps?

_____

_____

LESSON 3 • How Senses Work

Draw conclusions Why weren't you or your partner able to identify the objects unless the flaps were open?

_____
_____
_____

How did your results compare to your partner's results?

_____
_____
_____

Based on your results, make a **claim** about how sight, smell, and taste are involved in identifying things in your environment. Support your answer with **evidence** and **reasoning**.

_____
_____
_____
_____

Making Sense

How does your claim or the evidence you gathered in this investigation help you begin to explain how bats might use their senses to find food?

_____
_____
_____

EXPLORATION

Nerves and Receptors

Body Senses

Have you ever touched something hot with your hand? How did you react? You probably responded by pulling your hand back very quickly! Your body has **senses** that send you information about your environment. Together, your senses work together as a system to help you survive.

The Skeletal and Nervous Systems

Look at the image of body systems that work together. Then write the letter of each description near the system it describes.

a. Humans and many other animals have a **skeletal system** made mainly of bones. The skeletal system gives structure, support, and protection to the softer parts of the body.

b. The **nervous system** contains the **brain,** spinal cord, and nerves. The brain is the central processing organ. The skeletal system protects it.

c. The nervous system has two kinds of **nerves.** Some send information from parts of the body to the brain or spinal cord. Some send information from the brain and spinal cord to the rest of the body.

d. The **spinal cord** is a bundle of nerve fibers and tissues that connect the parts of the body to the brain. It is protected by the backbone. The brain and the spinal cord make up the central nervous system.

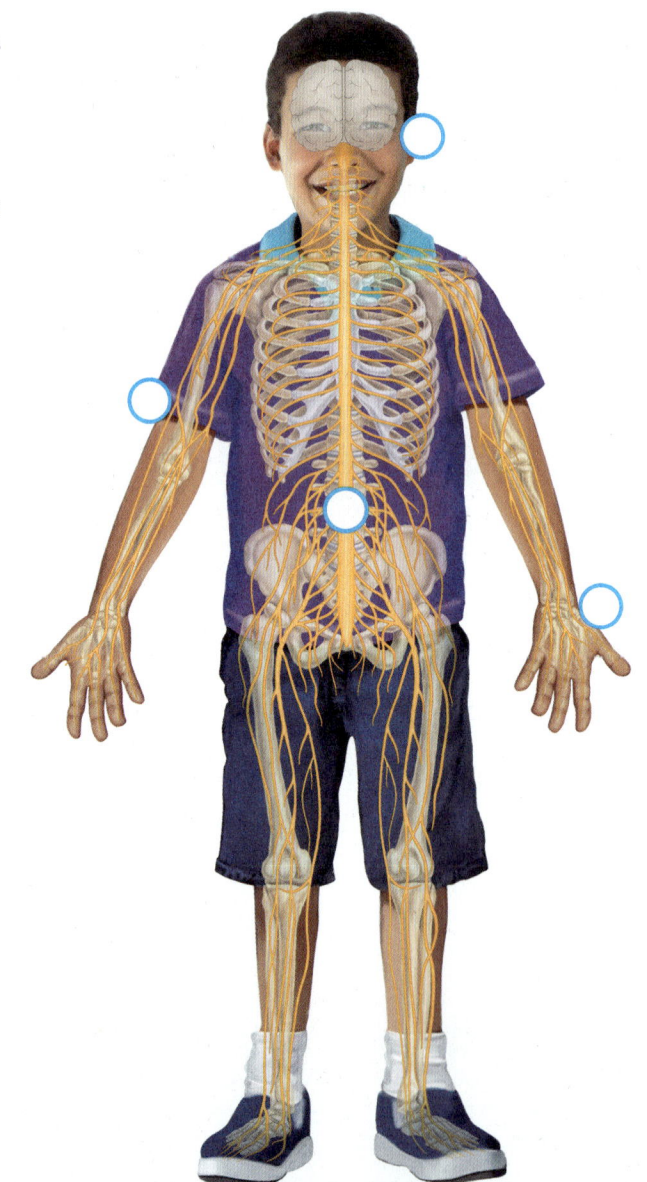

Skin Deep

The largest body organ is your skin. It covers and protects your entire body. Skin also contains special structures called **receptors.** Receptors respond to changes inside and outside the body, and they report these changes to your nervous system. The brain processes this information, forming perceptions and memories. Then these perceptions and memories can help guide your actions.

The ability to touch is one of your senses. Nerve endings on the skin or other surfaces of animals can receive different kinds of information from the environment. For example, skin receptors on a wing part of a insect-eating bat helps the bat sense and catch its prey.

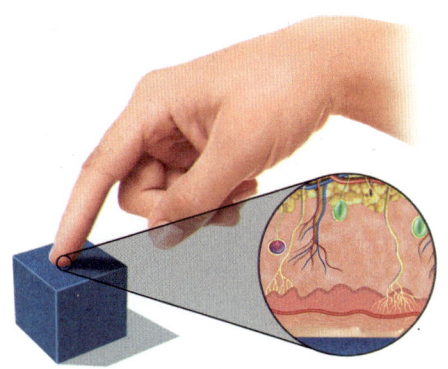

Touch and pressure receptors react to how hard, soft, rough, or smooth an object is. When you touch something such as a wood block, receptors send nerve signals to your brain. The brain processes these signals so that you know what you are touching.

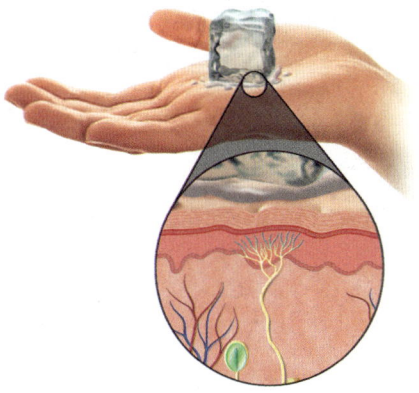

If you are holding an ice cube, you quickly realize that your hand is getting cold! Temperature receptors in your skin react to the temperature of the ice cube and send nerve signals to the brain.

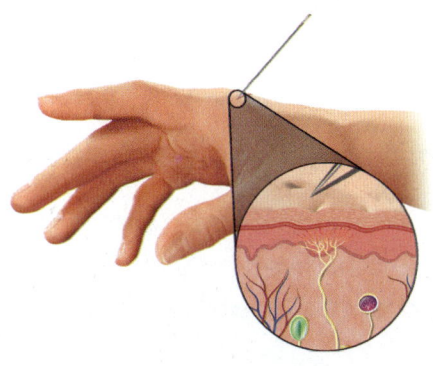

When the skin feels intense pressure or is injured, pain receptors send information about the pain to the central nervous system. The central nervous system processes the signals and causes the muscles to try to move away from the source of the pain. The body reacts immediately to pain.

Knee-Jerk Response

Not all sensory information travels to the brain to be processed. Has your doctor ever checked your reflexes?

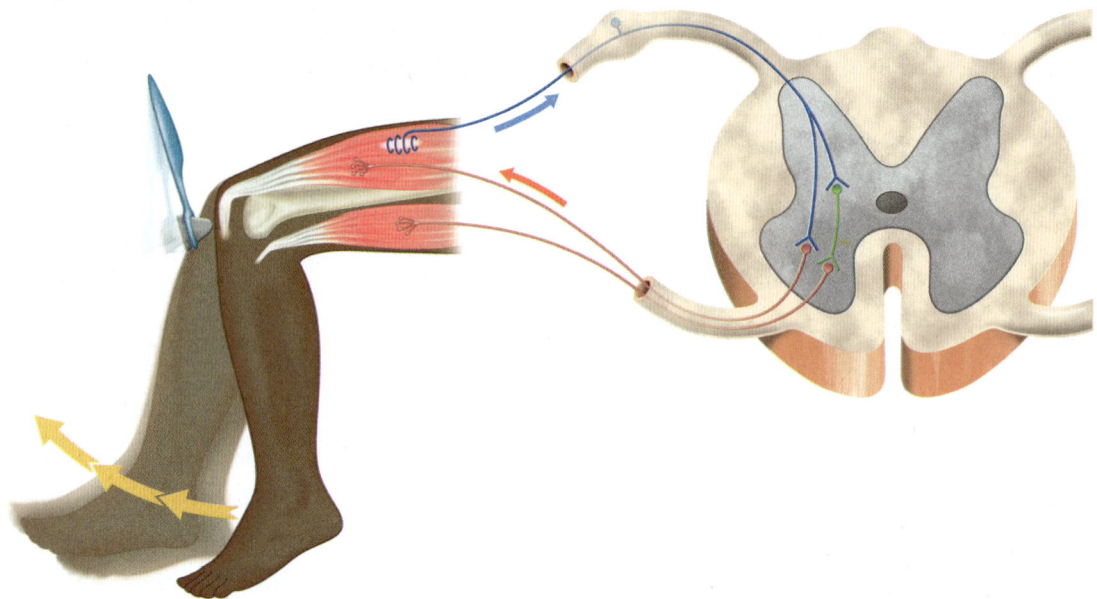

Certain body parts have receptors that send information to the spinal cord. From the spinal cord, a response is immediately sent back to the muscles. The brain is not involved. These reactions are called reflexes. Reflexes are important to many animals' survival because they allow animals to respond more quickly to their environment.

Making Sense

Using evidence from the text, construct an argument that describes the effects of bats using their senses to survive.

_____
_____
_____
_____

Discuss your answer with your group. Provide constructive feedback for each answer, and make sure everyone has a chance to speak.

EXPLORATION

Sights and Sounds

Eye See!

Along with the skin, tongue, and nose, there are also sensory receptors in the eyes. Many animals have specialized receptors that receive different types of information through the eyes. Your ability to see is another one of your senses.

If you have ever tried to find your way in the dark, you know how important light is for seeing. You are able to see because your eyes capture light and help turn it into an image, which is processed by the brain. When there is little light in a room, it is difficult to see objects inside that room. That's because eyes process light that is reflecting from objects. When there is plenty of light in a room, it is much easier to see objects inside that room. Eyes transmit the light they see to the brain as information.

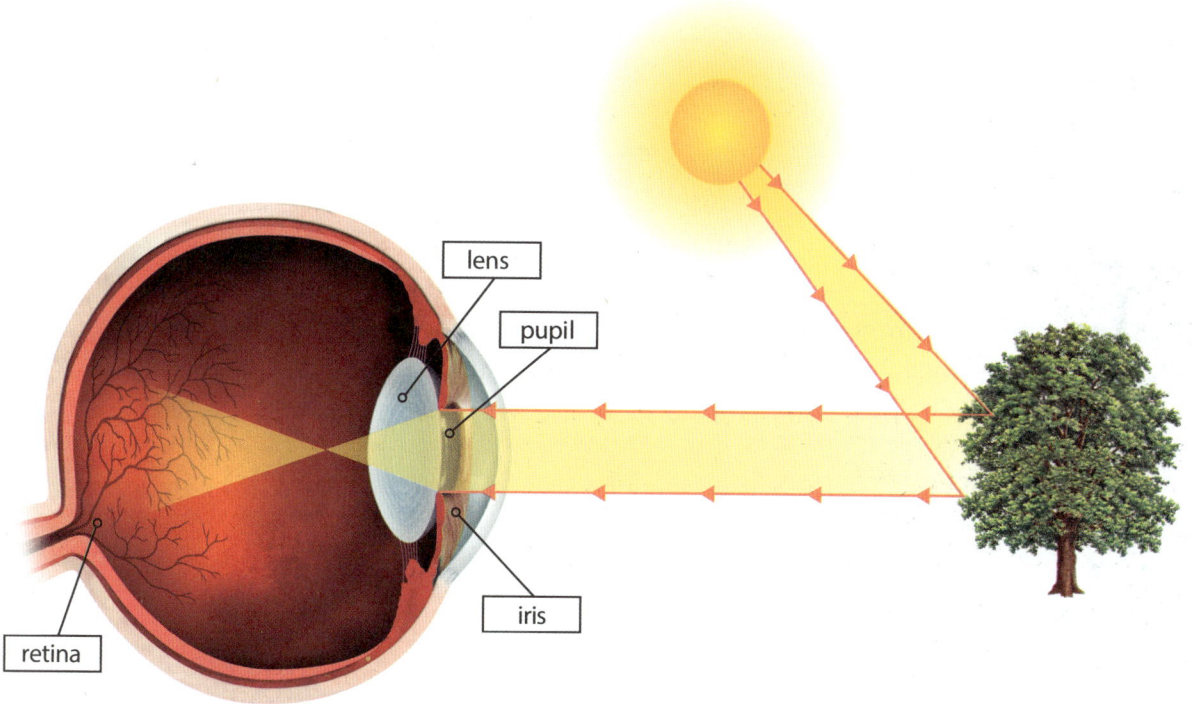

How does sight work? First, light bounces off an object, such as a tree. It then enters the eye through an opening at the center. After passing through the opening, light strikes the back of the eye. At the back of the eye is an area where there are light receptors. These receptors react to the light and send signals along a nerve pathway to the brain, where the information is processed. The information is stored in your brain as a memory. Then, the next time you see that object, you know what it is.

LESSON 3 • How Senses Work

Reflections of Light

Draw a model of the system that allows us to use light to see objects. Be sure to include a light source in your drawing.

Binocular Vision

Roll a piece of paper into a narrow tube. Then, hold one end of it to your eye. Now hold your free hand next to the tube in front of your other eye. Leave both eyes open. Look through the narrow tube with one eye. What do you see?

Most organisms have more than one eye. This allows some to have binocular vision. Binocular vision involves two eyes each seeing the same thing from a slightly different angle. This results in depth perception. Depth perception is the ability to see the world in three dimensions. It also allows organisms to judge how far away an object is.

Having two or more eyes allows the brain to better process visual information. By being able to judge how far away something is, animals can hunt for prey more easily. People can avoid dangers such as oncoming traffic or holes in the ground. Although you may have heard the phrase "blind as a bat," bats can actually see quite well. Their vision is particularly sensitive to low-light conditions. This sensitivity helps bats navigate to and from their roosting and feeding sites during dawn and dusk.

Here's to the Ears!

There are sounds everywhere, but you wouldn't be able to hear any of them without the hearing receptors in your ears. As you have learned, senses allow humans and other animals to receive different kinds of information. This information is carried by nerves to the brain. The brain processes the information, causing the body to react and respond to the information in different ways.

Animals have different levels of sensitivity to sound. Many animals can make and hear lower or higher sounds than humans can hear. For example, bats can hear sounds at frequencies 10 times higher than humans can hear.

All Ears

Explore the image that shows the parts of the ear and how they work together as a system. Then write the letter of each description near the part of the ear that is describe.

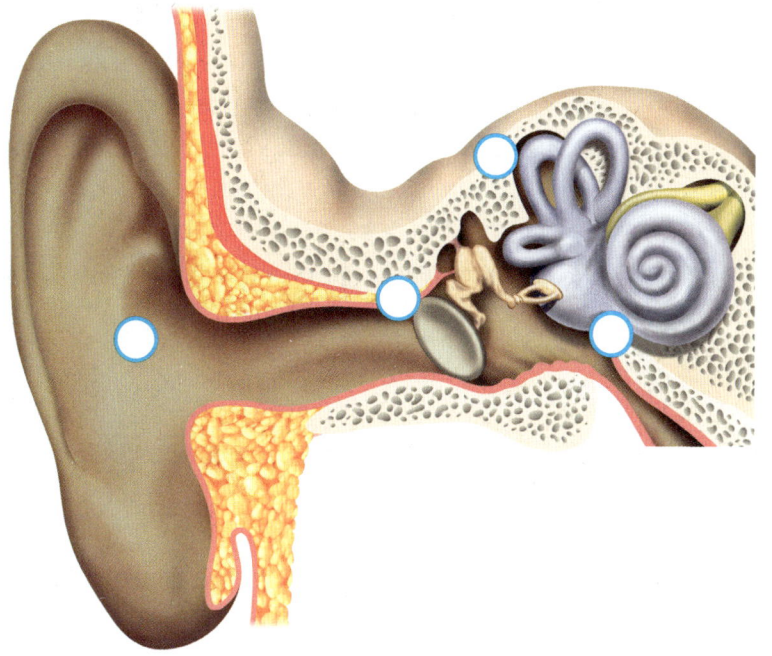

a. The **outer ear** is the part of the ear that you can see. The shape of the outer ear funnels sound into the ear, through the ear canal, and toward the middle ear.

b. The ear drum separates the outer ear from the **middle ear.** The middle ear is an air-filled area with three small bones: the hammer, the anvil, and the stirrup.

c. The **inner ear** contains the fluid-filled cochlea and the semicircular canals. The sound vibrations from the middle ear cause the fluid, as well as the thousands of tiny hairs inside the cochlea, to move.

d. The movement of tiny hairs inside the cochlea produce nerve signals that travel to the brain, where they are interpreted as sound.

"Seeing" By Hearing

Bats are the only flying mammals. As they fly, many bats send out sounds through their mouth and nose. When the sounds hit an object, the sounds bounce back, or echo, and are funneled into the bat's ears. As in humans, the sound vibrations move through the ear and are converted to signals sent along nerves to the brain. There the information is processed. Most bats use echolocation to locate food and to navigate while flying. Not all bats use echolocation. Flying fox bats, for example, find the fruits they eat using their sense of sight.

Making Sense

An animal's senses work together as a system to help them survive. Use evidence from this lesson to support that claim. How do your findings help you explain how bats use their senses to find food?

_____
_____
_____
_____

Name _____

Lesson Check

Can You Explain It?

Review your ideas from the beginning of this lesson about how bats use their senses to find food. How have your ideas changed? Be sure to do the following:

- Identify how bats use their five senses.
- Use data from the investigations and explorations to explain how senses work as a system.

Now I know or think that _____

_____

_____

_____

_____

_____

Making Connections

The elephant shrew has large eyes and ears. How might the shrew use its senses to find food and avoid predators? How is this similar to or different from the bat's behavior?

_____

_____

_____

_____

_____

Checkpoints

1. Match each situation to the kind of receptor that reacts.

watching a green lizard running	pain receptor
enjoying a sweet piece of fruit	sight receptor
feeling the poke of a sharp object	taste receptor

2. Use the image to help you choose the correct answer.

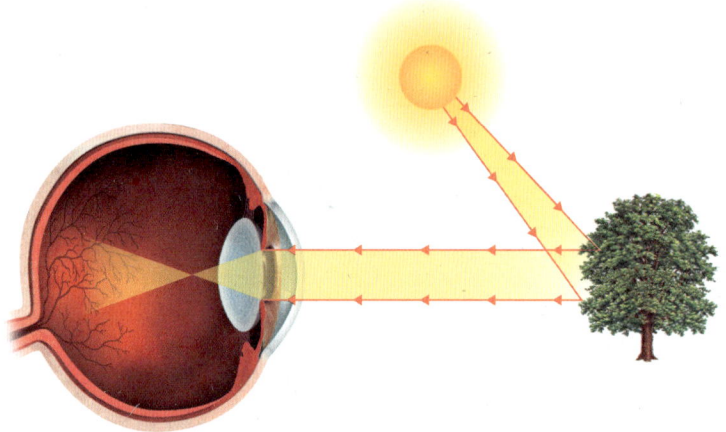

The eyes contain _____ receptors that react to light.

3. What would be a possible effect of holding your nose while eating your lunch? Circle the best answer.

  a. My lunch won't taste as good.
  b. I'll eat my lunch more quickly.
  c. My taste buds won't be able to function.
  d. The food in my lunch won't look the same.

4. How do sounds get from the inner ear to the brain? Circle all that apply.

  a. They pass through the eardrum.
  b. They make hairs move in the cochlea.
  c. They are translated by receptors into nerve signals.
  d. They cause fluid to move in the outer and middle ear.

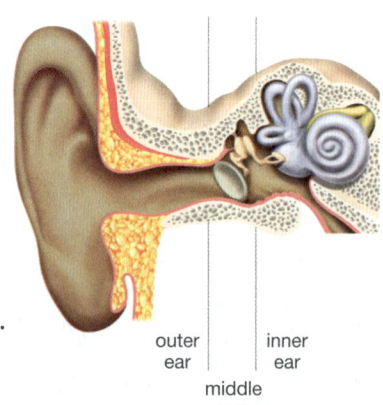

outer ear | middle ear | inner ear

5. Construct an argument using one or more of the phrases below to describe how a body system helps humans survive.

> skeletal system nervous system
> brain and spinal cord central nervous system

_____
_____
_____
_____
_____

6. Cheetahs use their sense of sight to find food during the day. Construct an argument to explain why a cheetah would have a hard time catching prey at night.

_____
_____
_____
_____
_____
_____

Name _____

Unit Review

1. Support the following **claim** with **evidence,** and support your **reasoning:** A leaf's function is to make food for the plant.

_____
_____
_____
_____
_____

2. Use an example to explain how a plant's systems work together to support the plant's survival, growth, or reproduction.

_____
_____
_____

3. Plants have different structures that are used for reproduction and for protection. Draw a model of a plant that has both structures, and identify if the structure is involved in reproduction or protection.

UNIT 2 • Plant and Animal Structure and Function

4. Which of the following qualities of a frog's skin is evidence that a frog is adapted to its environment? Circle all that apply.

   a. It is thin.
   b. It is slimy.
   c. It is warm.
   d. It is moist.

5. Classify each structure as mostly involved in protection (P) or motion (M):

   _____ fur
   _____ fins
   _____ legs
   _____ wings
   _____ shells
   _____ spines

6. Like bats, dolphins use echolocation to navigate and find food underwater. Circle which sense echolocation uses.

   a. taste
   b. touch
   c. smell
   d. hearing

7. Sophia plays basketball at her elementary school. She uses her brain, eyes, and nerves to play the sport. Use evidence to argue how these three parts of her body work together to manage her movements when she's trying to catch the ball.

_____
_____
_____
_____
_____

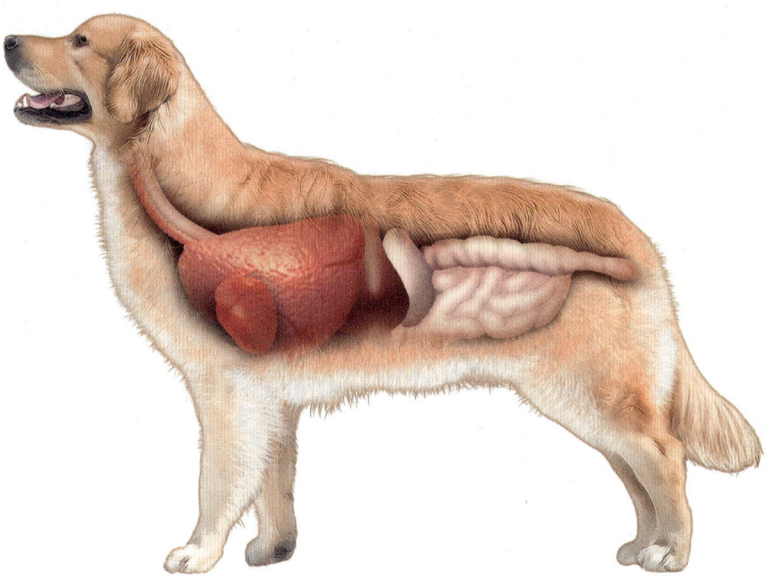

8. Support the following **claim** with **evidence,** and explain your **reasoning:** Animal systems have multiple parts that work together.

_____
_____
_____
_____

9. Ferns reproduce by forming spores. Explain how a fern's reproductive structure is different from that of an apple tree.

_____
_____
_____

10. Describe behavioral responses that plants have that cause them to react and grow in certain ways.

_____
_____
_____
_____

In Unit 2, you used models to determine how some systems in animals allow them to receive, process, and respond to information in the environment. In this unit, you will use models to discover how waves transfer energy and information and how that information is used by organisms, including people, to communicate across distances.

UNIT 3 Energy and Communication

Lesson 1
Energy Transfer and Transformation 88

Lesson 2
Collisions 108

Lesson 3
Waves 124

Lesson 4
Information Transfer 142

Unit Review 162

LESSON 1

Energy Transfer and Transformation

Rock on!

88 LESSON 1 • Energy Transfer and Transformation

What do you notice about these kids?

I notice _____

_____

_____

_____

What do you wonder about the band playing music?

I wonder _____

_____

_____

_____

Can You Explain It?

How does the band transfer and transform energy? Sketch, write, or model your answer.

LESSON 1 • Energy Transfer and Transformation

HANDS-ON ACTIVITY

Full of Energy

Energy is all around us. When you use your muscles to pick up a book, open a door, or toss a ball, you are using energy. Devices that use energy enable you to talk on the phone, watch programs, or get to school. **Energy** is the ability to cause change in matter.

Form a question Ask a question about how we use energy to do things.

> **Did you know?**
>
> The word energy comes from the Greek word *energeia*.

90 **LESSON 1** • Energy Transfer and Transformation

POSSIBLE MATERIALS
- [ ] safety goggles
- [ ] pinwheel
- [ ] bouncy balls
- [ ] wind-up cars
- [ ] popper or pop-up plastic toys
- [ ] tuning forks (different sizes)

STEP 1

Brainstorm With your group, discuss where you observed energy today, from the moment you woke up until you got to school. Make a list of your observations.

_____
_____
_____

STEP 2

Observe Your teacher will assign your group to a station where you will observe a system. As a group, you and your classmates will list the forms of energy you observe in each system. Wear your goggles, if necessary.

What is a system? What evidence will you look for to determine if energy is present?

_____
_____
_____

LESSON 1 • Energy Transfer and Transformation

STEP 3 **Organize your data** As you rotate through each station, record forms of energy you observe, changes in the interactions of the parts, and how energy transfers from one object to another or from place to place.

	Forms of energy observed	Transfers of energy from one object or place to another
Blowing on a pinwheel		
Pressing a popper or pop-up toy		
Winding a toy car		
Making a tuning fork vibrate		
Rolling a ball into another ball		

Make a **claim** about how energy is transferred. Cite **evidence** and explain your **reasoning**.

_____
_____
_____
_____
_____

Draw conclusions Compare your results with other groups in your class. What conclusions can you draw from the investigation?

_____

Making Sense

How do band members transfer energy to make music?

_____
_____
_____

When working in the stations, how did you make sure it was fair for everyone?

_____
_____

LESSON 1 • Energy Transfer and Transformation

HANDS-ON ACTIVITY

Light the Bulb

In a flashlight or other electrical device, a battery may be connected in a circuit. A **circuit** is a closed path or loop that an electric current flows through.

Form a question What questions do you have about how energy moves through a circuit?

_____
_____
_____
_____
_____

Did you know?

A bird can sit on power lines and not be electrocuted. However, if the bird also touches a second power line, it will close a circuit and be electrocuted.

POSSIBLE MATERIALS
- [ ] battery (size D) with holder
- [ ] light bulb with holder
- [ ] three lengths of wire
- [ ] switch

STEP 1 **Investigate your question** In the space below, plan a simple investigation to make the bulb light up.

STEP 2 **Make and test** Lay out the parts in the order you think will make the bulb light up. Connect the parts to test your plan. Draw and label a picture of how you connected all the parts.

LESSON 1 • Energy Transfer and Transformation

STEP 3 Does the bulb light up? If not, keep working until you "see the light!" What did you change about your arrangement?

_____
_____

After you've built a circuit that works, draw a picture of it. Show how the parts are connected.

Use **reasoning** to make a **claim** about circuits. Cite **evidence** to support your claim.

_____
_____

Making Sense

How does understanding circuits help you explain how energy is transferred and transformed by a band's electrical instruments?

_____
_____
_____
_____

LESSON 1 • Energy Transfer and Transformation

EXPLORATION

Energy Is All Around
Where Does Our Energy Come From?

When you turn on a television, you see pictures and hear sound. Where do the light and sound energy come from?

You can see a wire connecting a wall socket to the television. That wire carries electric current. **Electric current** is a flow of electric charges along a path. These photos show some of the steps in the system by which energy moves to your home.

How does electrical energy get to your home?

How do you use electrical energy?

Hundreds of millions of years ago, plants took in the sun's energy, just as they do now. After the plants died, a long, slow change turned them into coal. Some of the energy the plants got from the sun is now in that coal. That stored energy is called *chemical energy*.

Coal

 If you still don't understand how an electric current gets to your house, what should you do?

LESSON 1 • Energy Transfer and Transformation

Saving It for Later

A battery stores chemical energy. When a device uses the battery, the chemical energy inside the battery changes into electrical energy. The device changes the electrical energy into motion, sound, or other forms of energy. There are many types and sizes of batteries for different purposes.

Button batteries are named for their size and shape. They are small and reliable for devices that use small amounts of energy very slowly.

AA batteries are used in many devices. They come in both single-use and rechargeable forms.

9V batteries are useful in devices that change stored energy into other energy. This type of battery is a reliable energy source for safety devices.

Transfer to Transform

We observe energy changes every day. Think about where the energy comes from and where the energy goes.

In a flashlight, the chemical energy in a battery is *transformed* into electrical energy. This energy is *transferred* to the light bulb, which *transforms* it into light energy.

98   LESSON 1 • Energy Transfer and Transformation

Electrical energy *transfers* into a cell phone. The electrical energy is *transformed* into sound energy by the phone, which allows you to have a conversation. Does it *transform* into another type of energy?

You walk into a dark room, flip a switch, and a lamp turns on. What kind of energy from the lamp allows you to see? How did energy change from one form to another?

The switch allows electrical energy to flow through the lamp cord and into the lamp. This is an **energy transfer**, a movement of energy from place to place or from object to object.

Inside the lamp, electrical energy is transferred to the light bulb. The bulb transforms the electrical energy into light energy. **Energy transformation** is a change in energy from one form to another. Which other type of energy does the light bulb transform electricity into?

Heat! A light bulb transforms electricity into light and heat. When electrical energy transfers into a device, the energy usually transforms into more than one form of energy.

In a drone, chemical energy inside the battery is *transformed* into electrical energy. This electrical energy is *transferred* to the drone's propellers. Then, the electrical energy *transforms* into motion and sound energy when the drone flies.

LESSON 1 • Energy Transfer and Transformation   99

Changing Forms of Energy

Have you ever used a laptop computer and had the battery "die"? Why do laptop batteries need to be recharged so often?

Right after being plugged in and recharged, a laptop's battery indicator shows a full charge. After the laptop has been used a lot, the energy stored in the battery is nearly gone.

When a laptop is active, its stored energy is being used. Typing a document uses energy. Playing games can use a great deal of energy. Where does this energy come from?

Stored chemical energy in the laptop battery is transformed into electrical energy. The laptop can then transform this electrical energy into light, sound, and heat.

When you see an example of energy such as a warm bowl of soup, you know the energy was transferred from somewhere else. You also know that the energy will eventually transfer or change form. The soup will cool off, warming the air around it. Energy can move and change, but it does not disappear or get destroyed.

Making Sense

Engineers have improved technology over time to store energy more efficiently and effectively. Explain how this improved technology allows the electrical instruments in a band to transfer and transform energy.

EXPLORATION

Heat

Hot or Not?

How do we know if something is cold or hot? Sometimes, we can see clues. The terms *hot* and *cold* are ways to describe temperature. These photos show evidence of energy transfer as heat.

Dry ice is a solid form of carbon dioxide. Carbon dioxide freezes at a much colder temperature than water.

Glassblowing involves high temperatures. Glass is heated to the point that it becomes molten. It can then be shaped.

Hot by Contact

Heat is energy that transfers between objects with different temperatures. Heat energy sometimes transfers easily between objects that are touching. When objects of two different temperatures touch, energy as heat moves from the warmer object to the cooler object.

Energy is transferred as heat moves from a stove burner to a skillet.

Energy is also transferred as heat moves from the hot skillet to the colder pancake batter.

LESSON 1 • Energy Transfer and Transformation

Distant Heat

Pancakes cook because objects touch each other. The transfer of energy as heat can also occur between objects that are not touching each other.

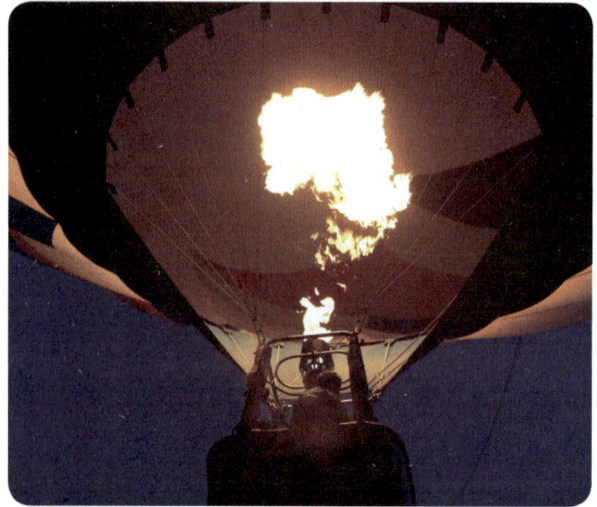

In a hot-air balloon, the flame of a gas burner warms the air above it. The hot air rises into the balloon. Soon the whole balloon is full of hot air.

A space heater transfers energy as heat to the air around it. Soon, the whole room is nice and warm.

Remember that heat moves from something warmer to something cooler. You rely on this process every day. Sometimes you can feel heat from something that wasn't near a fire or heater. For example, have you ever touched an electronic charger or held your hand close to a light bulb? It felt warm because some of the electrical energy that causes the device to work was transformed into heat energy.

Making Sense

Now that you have explored how energy can be transferred as heat, how do your findings help you explain why a music band might need an electric fan to cool their equipment?

EXPLORATION

Energy of Sound

Sound All Around

Sounds are all around you. But what is sound?

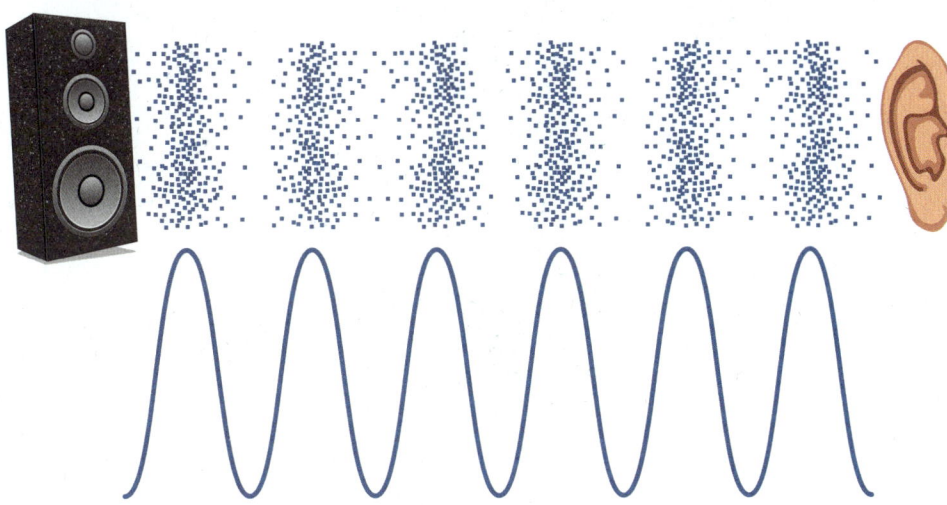

You can't see sound waves. But the small particles that make up all kinds of matter vibrate as sound waves strike objects.

Sound is the movement of energy through vibrations. To vibrate means "to move back and forth." Sound vibrations come from an object or organism that starts the vibration. Then the vibration travels through the air or surrounding objects. When a sound vibration reaches your ear, you sense the sound.

When you pluck a guitar string, it vibrates. If you pluck it hard, you transfer a lot of energy to the string. The sound is loud. If you pluck it softly, you transfer less energy.

Telephones, televisions, radios, and computers all have speakers. Speakers transform electrical energy into vibrations. A speaker vibrates and transfers sound energy through the air to your ear.

LESSON 1 • Energy Transfer and Transformation

Loud and Soft, High and Low

Sounds are everywhere. Some sounds, such as whispers, are soft. Other sounds, such as fireworks and thunder, are very loud.

An airplane's engines roar as the plane takes off and touches down. The airplane makes a loud sound, which is a great deal of energy.

A mouse is a small animal that makes squeaky sounds. A mouse makes a soft sound when it squeaks, which is less energy than the plane.

Why do sounds differ? It's because of energy transfer. If a lot of energy is transferred from or to an object, the sound is loud. If less energy is transferred from or to an object, the sound is softer. Loud sounds have more energy than softer sounds.

 Sometimes loud noises bother people. With a partner, discuss how you could support someone who is affected by loud sounds.

Making Sense

How do band members use their voices and a microphone to transform and transfer energy to make sound?

_____
_____
_____

104 LESSON 1 • Energy Transfer and Transformation

Name _____

Lesson Check

Can You Explain It?

You have learned about energy and how one form can be changed into another. Review your ideas from the beginning of this lesson about how energy is transferred and transformed. How have your ideas changed?

Be sure to do the following:
- Define energy transfer.
- Explain the evidence from the photo of a band that shows energy is being transferred and transformed.

Now I know or think that _____

_____

_____

_____

Making Connections

When you toast bread, it changes color and temperature. How is this similar to energy transfer and transformation made by a band playing music?

_____

_____

_____

_____

LESSON 1 • Energy Transfer and Transformation

Checkpoints

1. Which of these devices does NOT change electrical energy into motion energy? Choose the best answer.
   a. DVD player
   b. clock
   c. clothes dryer
   d. electric light

2. Which form of energy can easily be observed in all of these: a washing machine, a printer, and a radio? Choose the best answer.
   a. sound
   b. motion
   c. chemical
   d. heat

3. Which of the following are evidence of energy transfer involving sound? Circle all that apply.
   a. a lit bulb
   b. an airplane taking off
   c. water dripping
   d. an orchestra playing music
   e. a solar cooker in use
   f. kids whispering
   g. an ice pack in use

4. You have a new toy that needs batteries. On the lines below, plan and describe how you would investigate whether energy is transferred and transformed when the toy is turned on.

   _____
   _____
   _____
   _____

5. What is the source of the energy for the microwave? Explain how you know heat was involved in cooking the broccoli.

_____

_____

_____

_____

_____

6. In the space below, draw a model that shows energy being transferred and transformed. Label the model and identify the forms of energy.

LESSON 2
Collisions

What do you notice about the wrecking ball and the wall?

I notice _____

_____

_____

_____

What do you wonder about the wrecking ball and the wall?

I wonder _____

_____

_____

_____

Can You Explain It?

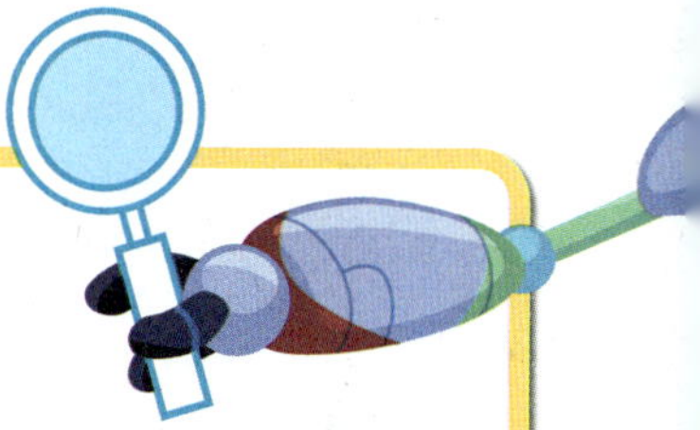

Why does the wall move when it is hit by the wrecking ball? Sketch, write or model your answer.

_____

_____

_____

_____

_____

_____

_____

LESSON 2 • Collisions

HANDS-ON ACTIVITY

Test It! Stored Energy in a Rubber Band

Look at the pole vaulter. Pole vaulters start by running while holding the pole. Then, they plant the bottom of the pole, arch their bodies, and push themselves over the bar. While they do this, the pole bends without breaking. The bend in the pole stores energy that is transferred to vaulters and lifts them over the bar.

Form a question Ask a question about how energy can be stored.

_____
_____
_____
_____

Did you know?

The highest pole vault recorded was 20 ft 2.5 in.

POSSIBLE MATERIALS
- [ ] safety goggles
- [ ] giant rubber band
- [ ] chair
- [ ] 2 metersticks
- [ ] toy car or truck
- [ ] index card
- [ ] ruler

STEP 1 CAUTION: Wear safety goggles. Stretch the rubber band so it wraps around the front legs of the chair. Place two metersticks in front of the chair. They should be 20 cm apart and in parallel lines to serve as a track for the toy car or truck.

What role does the rubber band play in this investigation?

_____

_____

STEP 2 Tape an index card to the floor behind the rubber band. Use a ruler to mark lines on the card that are 2 cm and 4 cm behind the rubber band. Choose a third distance and mark it.

What do the marks represent? Why are they important?

_____

_____

LESSON 2 • Collisions

STEP 3 **Investigate your question** How can you use this device to investigate the question that you formed at the beginning of this activity? Think about the materials available and what else you might need. Write your investigation plan on a separate sheet of paper. Show it to your teacher if you need additional materials.

 How are you communicating with your group during this activity? Turn to a partner and discuss how to better communicate to gather evidence.

STEP 4 **Organize your data** Carry out your plan and record your results. You can use the space below to make a table to record your data.

STEP 5

Share Decide how to present your data to show what you did and what happened. You may wish to use a table or graph as a presentation tool.

What happened when you applied more energy to the rubber band? What happened when you applied less energy to the rubber band?

_____

_____

_____

Compare your investigation and results to other groups' findings. Do their findings support yours? What conclusions can you draw from this?

_____

_____

Make a **claim** about how much stored energy exists in a rubber band based on your experiment. Cite **evidence** to support your **reasoning**.

_____

_____

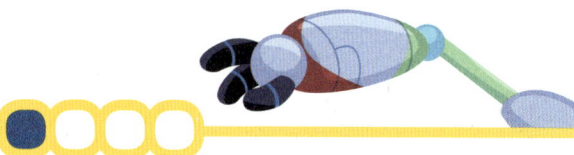

Making Sense

How does this activity help you begin to explain why the wall collapses when it is hit with the wrecking ball?

_____

_____

_____

LESSON 2 • Collisions

HANDS-ON ACTIVITY

Speed and Energy

A baseball pitcher throws the ball toward a hitter. When the hitter's bat makes contact with the ball, the ball changes direction. Energy is transferred and transformed when the bat collides with the ball.

Form a question Ask a question about speed and energy.

Did you know?

It was reported that one of the longest home runs ever hit in baseball was around 177 m (582 ft)!

POSSIBLE MATERIALS
- [ ] string
- [ ] medium wooden block
- [ ] masking tape
- [ ] large plastic cup

STEP 1

Investigate your question Tie the end of the string around the wooden block. There should be about 30 cm of string left untied. Place a piece of masking tape in the middle of the left-hand side of your desk. Place the cup upside down on top of the piece of tape.

Hold the untied end of the string with the block hanging down beside the upside-down cup. Pull the block back a few centimeters and let go. What happens to the cup?

 Sometimes following instructions is tricky. If you don't understand how to do something, what should you do? Share your ideas with your group.

LESSON 2 • Collisions

STEP 2 **Draw conclusions** Pull the block back a little farther than you did in Step 1 and let go. How does the movement of the cup compare to the previous step? Repeat Step 2 two more times, each time pulling the block back farther. How does the movement of the cup compare to the previous times?

_____
_____
_____

Make a **claim** about how the speed of the wooden block affects the cup when the block and cup collide. Support your claim with **evidence** from your investigation and explain your **reasoning.**

_____
_____
_____
_____

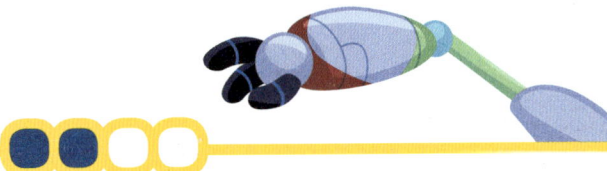

Making Sense

How does the evidence you gathered help you understand how the speed of a wrecking ball affects how much damage is done to a wall?

_____
_____
_____
_____

LESSON 2 • Collisions

EXPLORATION

Things That Move Have Energy

What do a moving car and a stretched rubber band being released have in common? They have motion energy! Anything moving has motion energy. Objects can also have stored energy because of their position. The energy of a roller coaster on a hill becomes motion when it races down!

There might be a dish on the edge of a shelf, ready to fall. Even before the dish falls, it has energy because of its position up on the shelf.

When you swing on a swing set, you have motion energy. At the top of each swing, you stop moving but have stored energy to move again.

When an archer pulls back on the string to shoot an arrow, energy is being stored. What will happen when the archer lets go of the string?

A rolling soccer ball has motion energy. Kicking it adds to that energy, making the ball move even faster, so the player can score a goal!

LESSON 2 • Collisions

Swifter and Stronger!

You observed in the hands-on activity that the faster you swung the wooden block, the more energy it had. The increased energy made the cup move more. Is the same true for bowling balls and bowling pins? Let's find out!

Slide a bowling ball slowly toward the pins.
....

When the ball hits the pins, how many pins fall down? Do they topple over or fly from the other pins?
....

Now move the ball faster. How many pins fall?
....

What else do you notice about the pins when a fast ball hits them?
....

Making Sense

How does knowing about the energy of things that move help you explain how the wrecking ball does damage to the wall?

EXPLORATION

Collisions
Crashing Dummies

What is a collision? A **collision** happens when two objects bump into each other. The result of a collision is a force being applied to the two things that collide.

Would you rather collide with something moving quickly or slowly? A slow-moving object has less energy, so the collision has less of an impact. A fast-moving object has more energy—so it makes a much bigger impact.

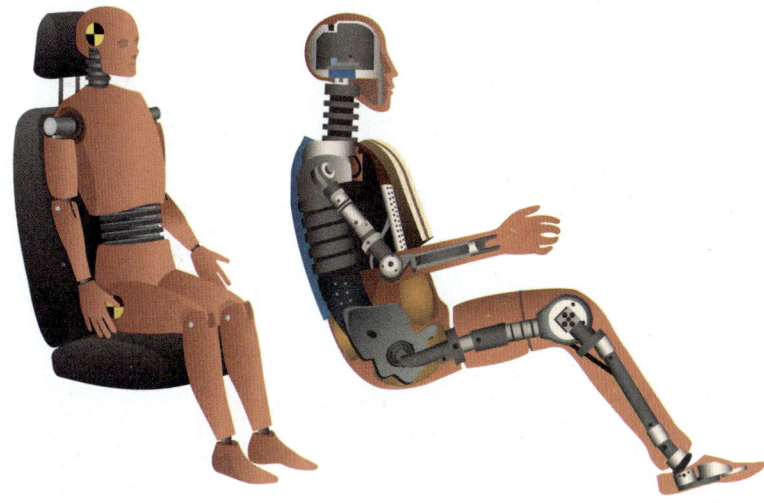

This crash-test dummy is built to the size and weight of a human.

The dummy contains sensors. These record how energy from a car's motion changes and affects the body.

Car accidents are a type of collision, and engineers try to minimize their impacts. After they make and build a design, they test it for safety using crash-test dummies.

Using dummies gives engineers a lot of information about what can happen in a collision, but without hurting anyone. These tests allow the engineers to evaluate vehicle safety.

Energy from a slow collision is absorbed by the car and body. Some is transferred as sound.

In a high-speed collision, crash-test dummies suffer more damage.

 It is important to be safe when at home and school. Share with a friend ways that you stay safe while at school.

LESSON 2 • Collisions

Too Hot to Handle!

Have you ever hit a nail with a hammer? That collision makes a lot of noise! If you touched the nail after hammering it, you would notice the nail was warm. The hammer would be warm, too! What causes the nail and hammer to heat up? When energy moves between objects, it can be transformed into heat, sound, motion, or other forms of energy.

When a hammer and nail collide, the energy is transformed into heat, sound and motion.

Making Sense

Describe how you know that energy is transferred when a wrecking ball collides with a wall. What is your evidence?

Name _____

Lesson Check

Can You Explain It?

What happens when the wrecking ball hits the wall? Write a few sentences below to explain what happens to the wall.

Be sure to do the following:
- Describe the motion and collisions.
- Identify energy movement.
- Mention heat or sound.

Now I know or think that _____

_____

_____

_____

Making Connections

How are these falling blocks similar to the wrecking ball and wall?

_____

_____

_____

_____

LESSON 2 • Collisions 121

Checkpoints

1. A soccer ball sits in the grass. A girl pulls her leg back to kick the soccer ball. She kicks! How does the transfer of energy affect the movement of the ball? Circle all the correct answers.

    a. The ball travels in one direction while the leg continues to move.

    b. The ball travels in one direction while the leg stops.

    c. The collision of the leg and ball makes the ball travel quickly.

    d. The collision of the leg and ball produces a noise.

    e. The ball travels forward while the leg moves backward.

2. Explain how an engineer might use a crash-test dummy to improve vehicle safety.

    _____

    _____

    _____

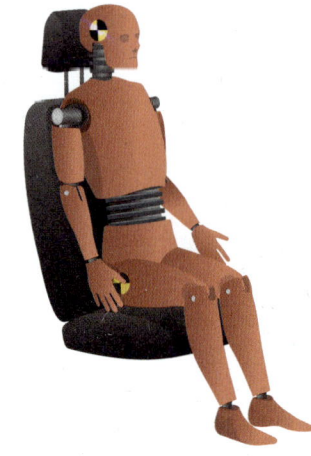

3. A roller coaster moves to the top of a hill, where it stops. What happens to the energy when the coaster stops?

    a. The energy becomes motion energy.

    b. The energy is stored energy.

    c. The energy converts to heat energy.

    d. The energy transfers to the tracks.

4. An archer is shooting an arrow with a bow. He pulls the string far back, lets the arrow go, and watches it fly far. On his second try, he uses a lighter arrow while pulling the string back the same distance as before. Tell what happens next. How do you know?

    _____

    _____

    _____

    _____

5. Explain what happens when you swing a ball and it collides with a gong. How does speed affect how the gong reacts?

_____

_____

_____

_____

6. What happens to a bowling ball when it collides with the pins? Circle all that apply.

   a. It changes direction.

   b. It gains stored energy.

   c. It gains energy of motion.

   d. It loses some of its energy.

7. You and a friend are sitting on the ground a few meters apart. You each have a basketball that you roll toward each other. The ball that your friend rolls is moving faster. Write a few sentences to tell what happens next.

_____

_____

_____

8. Make a claim about how an athlete uses a collision to transfer energy to change the direction of an object. Support your claim with evidence.

_____

_____

_____

LESSON 3
Waves

Cowabunga!

124 LESSON 3 • Waves

What do you notice about the surfer?

I notice _____

_____

_____

_____

What do you wonder about how the surfer moves through the water?

I wonder _____

_____

_____

_____

Can You Explain It?

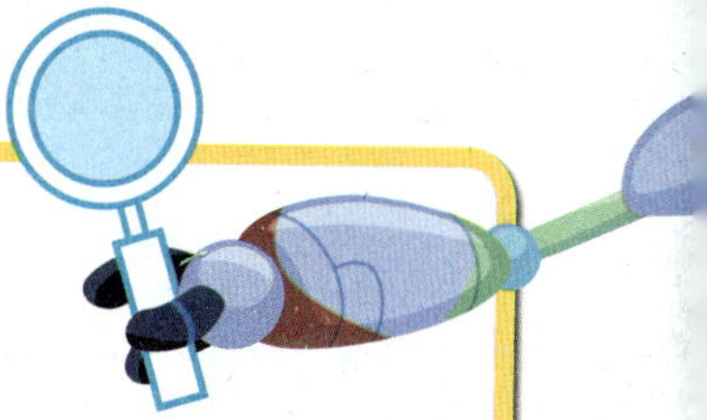

How does the wave move the surfer? Sketch, write, or model your answer.

_____

_____

_____

_____

_____

_____

_____

_____

LESSON 3 • Waves

HANDS-ON ACTIVITY

Let's Make Waves!

You may see and experience waves every day. One kind of wave is the up-and-down movement of water. Wind can make a flag wave. In science, a **wave** is a disturbance that carries energy, such as sound or light.

Form a question Ask a question about waves.

_____
_____
_____
_____

Did you know?
The largest wave recorded peaked at about 524 m (1,720 ft).

POSSIBLE MATERIALS

- [ ] aluminum pan
- [ ] water
- [ ] table tennis ball
- [ ] shoebox
- [ ] speaker or smartphone
- [ ] puffed rice
- [ ] large round cloth

STEP 1 Fill the aluminum pan with water. Place a table tennis ball at one end of the pan. Tap the water. Observe the ball. What happens to the ball? What causes this to occur?

_____

_____

_____

STEP 2 Place a shoebox over a small speaker with the volume turned up. Pour a handful of puffed rice on top of the shoebox. Play music. Observe the puffed rice. What is happening to the rice? Do you notice any patterns?

_____

_____

 Does everyone have to agree on the same ideas? Why or why not? Share your thoughts with the group.

LESSON 3 • Waves

STEP 3 With partners, hold the edges of a large, round cloth. Have everyone hold the cloth at a low, level height. One person should quickly raise and lower their section of the cloth. Observe what happens to the cloth. What happened to the motion in the cloth?

What kinds of mediums did you make waves in?

_____

How did the waves move in each of your investigations?

_____
_____

Make a **claim** about how waves affect other objects. Cite your **evidence** and explain your **reasoning**.

_____
_____

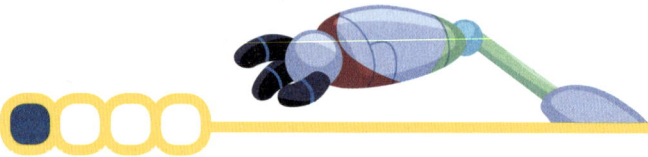

Making Sense

How does your claim or evidence you gathered in this investigation help you begin to understand how the surfer moves through the water?

_____
_____
_____
_____

LESSON 3 • Waves

HANDS-ON ACTIVITY

Bobbing and Waving

Sometimes, out at sea, strong winds or heavy storms create large waves that have a lot of energy. These waves can travel great distances until they find a place to release all that energy. Some buoys measure and collect data about this energy. They move up and down with the waves but do not move forward from their spots.

Form a question Ask a question about how waves affect buoys.

_____
_____
_____
_____

Did you know?

The Pacific Ocean is the largest and deepest ocean on Earth.

LESSON 3 • Waves   129

POSSIBLE MATERIALS
- [ ] clear plastic container
- [ ] water
- [ ] cork

STEP 1 **Investigate your question**
Get a container and a cork from your teacher. Fill the container up part of the way with water, and drop the cork into it. What do you observe with the water and cork?

_____
_____

STEP 2 Gently rock the container side to side to add more energy to the water. Record your observations of the water in the container in terms of energy.

_____
_____

Making Sense

Think about the surfer from the beginning of the lesson. How do the waves move the cork? How is that similar to the surfer?

_____
_____
_____
_____

130 LESSON 3 • Waves

EXPLORATION

How Waves Transfer Energy

Waves 101

When you throw a rock into the water, it creates ripples. Ripples form because the motion energy of the rock is transferred to the water. Waves are evidence that energy is transferred.

A wave's size is related to the amount of energy that is transferred. The photo shows what happened when a small rock was dropped into a pond.

Ocean Waves and Energy Transfer

Waves in the ocean can carry a lot of energy.

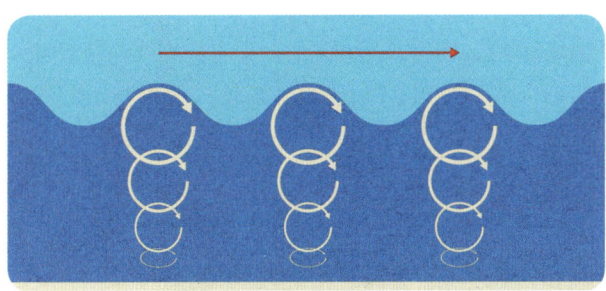

Wind transfers energy to the ocean's surface, causing a wave to form. Each circle shows the movement of water up and around in a wave. The water doesn't move forward. Only the wave energy moves forward.

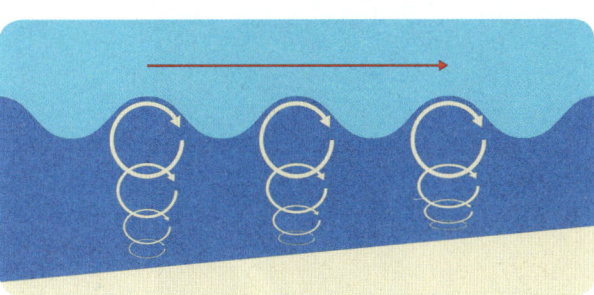

As the water becomes shallower, the water has less room to move, which forces it to move higher into the air. The height of the wave increases, and the energy moves forward more slowly.

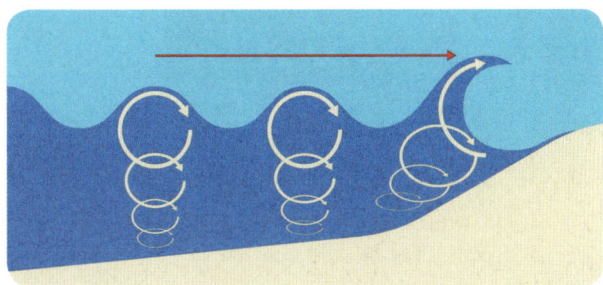

When a wave gets close to the beach, the back of the wave moves faster than the front, causing the wave to break. As the water crashes onto the shore, some of the energy produces sound, and some causes beach erosion.

Waves That Move Up and Down

A wave transfers energy in the direction it travels. But the matter it travels through may not move in the same direction as the wave.

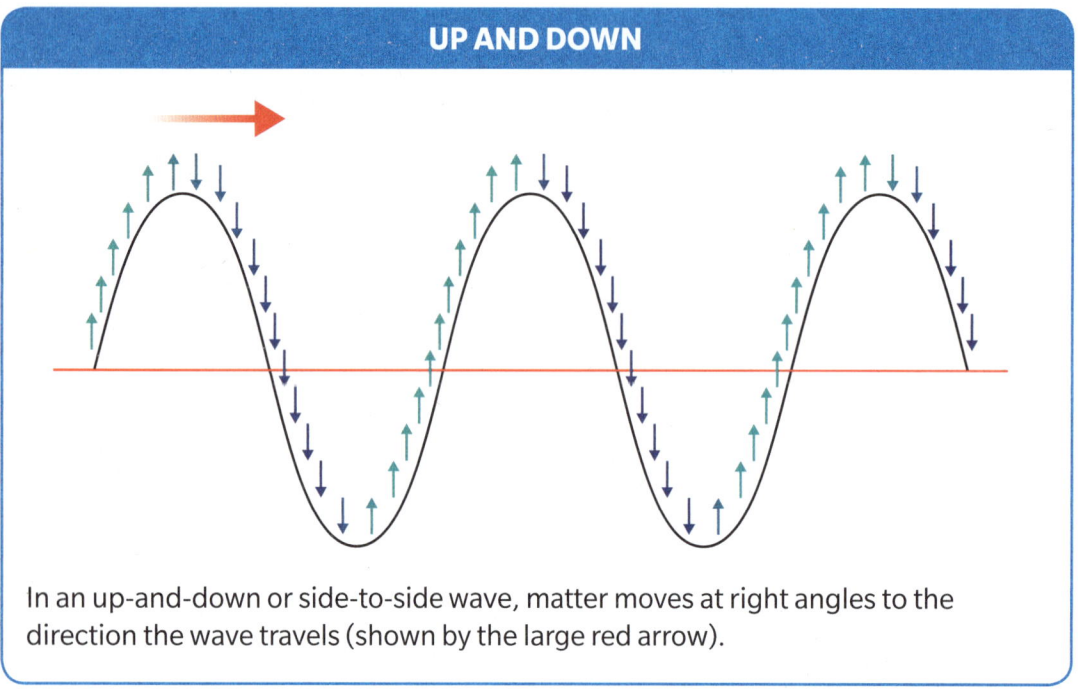

UP AND DOWN

In an up-and-down or side-to-side wave, matter moves at right angles to the direction the wave travels (shown by the large red arrow).

Waves that move up and down or side to side are very common. They can move through all types of matter and even through empty space.

A buoy bobs up and down in the water as waves pass by. If you know which way the waves are moving, you can tell which way the energy in the water is moving.

Signals from satellites, such as this one, travel through the vacuum of space and through clouds and the air to reach Earth's surface. These waves move at the same speed as sunlight.

132 LESSON 3 • Waves

Shake Like a Quake!

BOOM! A firework goes off! There's a bright flash of light followed by the sound of an explosion. Light and sound are both waves. But with sound, matter moves differently.

BACK AND FORTH

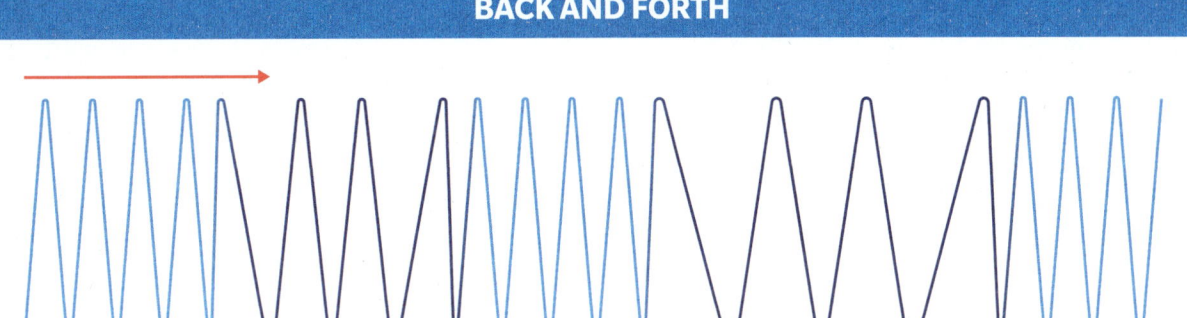

The wave travels to the right. The particles of the medium move back and forth in the same direction the wave travels, or parallel to the wave.

Sound is one example of a wave in which energy and matter move in the same direction. Unlike light, sound can only travel through matter. Sound travels better through water than through air. Because of this, animals that live in the ocean can hear sounds that are far away from them.

When someone strikes a drum, the drum's skin vibrates. Sound waves traveling away from the drumhead compress and expand the air in bands. In this way, sound energy travels to our ears.

Music can help people feel better if they are sad, scared, or mad. Share a time when music has helped change your mood.

LESSON 3 • Waves   133

Earthquakes can cause a lot of damage.

Waves generated during an earthquake also move back and forth. When the ground starts to shake during a quake, different waves move through the rocks in the ground. Scientists study these waves to figure out how strong an earthquake is.

A wave that moves through the ground is known as a seismic wave. Seismic waves that travel along the surface of Earth are responsible for most earthquake damage.

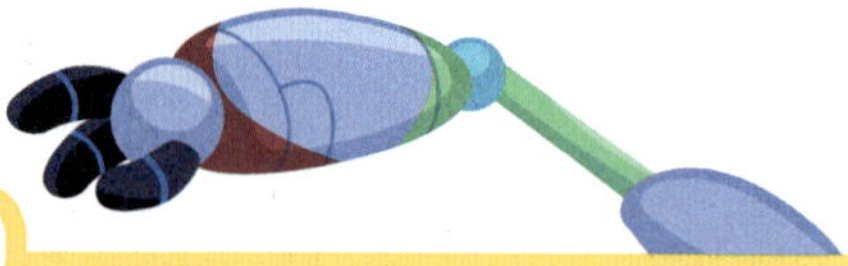

Making Sense

How does the evidence you gathered help you understand how the energy in a wave can make a surfer move?

_____

_____

LESSON 3 • Waves

EXPLORATION

Wave Parts

Waves have different parts.

The top of a wave is called a **crest**. This is the highest point on a wave. The crest is where matter is moved the farthest upward.

The bottom of a wave is called a **trough**. This is the lowest point on a wave. The trough is where matter is moved the farthest downward.

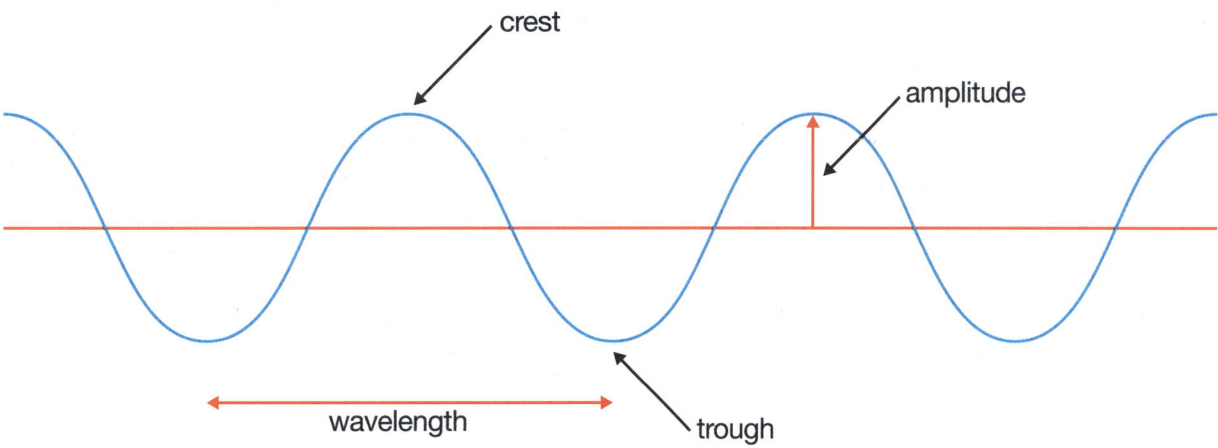

The distance between neighboring crests or troughs is called the **wavelength**. The wavelength is the distance between a point on one wave and the same point on the next wave. Wavelengths are described as short or long.

The height of a wave is called its **amplitude**. The amplitude is half the distance from the crest to the trough. Waves with a greater amplitude have more energy than waves with a lower amplitude.

 How could you and another classmate work together to model waves with your arms?

_____

_____

LESSON 3 • Waves   135

Can You Hear This?

All waves have an amplitude and a wavelength. In a sound wave, the amplitude is related to how loud something is. Loudness is also called **volume.** Compare the sounds described on this page to learn how amplitude differs for different sounds.

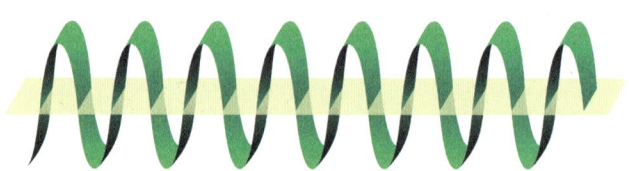

Engines on a jet produce very loud sounds. These sound waves have a lot of energy that is carried over a long distance.

The amplitude of a sound wave produced by a jet engine is very large. The distance between the crest and trough is large.

Songbirds produce soft sounds when they chirp. These sounds can only be heard over a short distance because they have a small amount of energy.

The amplitude of a sound wave produced by a songbird is small. The distance between the crest and trough is small.

Sound waves with more energy and volume have larger amplitudes. Sound waves with less energy and volume have smaller amplitudes. Compare the sounds described below to learn how wavelength differs.

A dog whistle produces sound waves that only dogs and some other types of animals can hear.

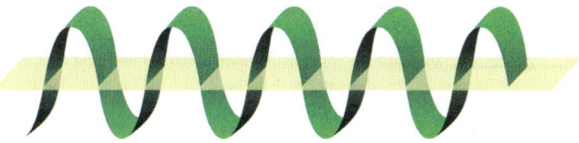

The wavelength of a sound produced by a dog whistle is short. The distance between two neighboring crests is small.

A flute produces a variety of sound waves that humans can hear.

The wavelength of a sound produced by a flute is longer than the wavelength produced by a dog whistle.

Remember the surfer from the beginning of the lesson? Let's use what you have discovered about the parts of a wave to explain what happens when someone surfs on a wave. Like all waves, ocean waves have amplitudes and wavelengths. Look at the images of the beach. When should the surfer choose to ride? Circle that image.

The wavelengths are short. The amplitude is low.

The wave amplitude has increased. Crests are high, and the wavelengths are long.

Making Sense

How does the evidence you gathered help you understand how the parts of a wave help the surfer balance?

Name _____

Lesson Check

Can You Explain It?

Now that you have learned about waves, explain how a surfer gets onto a wave.

Be sure to do the following:

- Explain how waves carry energy.
- Identify the properties and parts of waves.

Now I know or think that _____

_____

_____

_____

_____

Making Connections

How are the waves in the parachute moving the ball? How is this similar to the waves that surfers ride?

_____

_____

_____

_____

LESSON 3 • Waves   139

Checkpoints

1. What would happen to the pattern of waves in a pond if a large rock was dropped into the water?

    a. The waves would be closer together.

    b. The waves would be smaller.

    c. There would be fewer waves with less energy.

    d. There would be larger waves with more energy.

2. Look at the picture of ocean waves. Imagine you are in the ocean, and the water reaches your waist. How will energy in a small wave affect you as the wave passes by?

_____

_____

_____

_____

3. Scientists use a tool that records an earthquake's seismic waves. Suppose this tool records waves that have a very high amplitude. What can you conclude about the strength of the earthquake? Explain.

_____

_____

_____

_____

_____

4. Label each part of the wave.
   a. crest
   b. trough
   c. wavelength
   d. amplitude

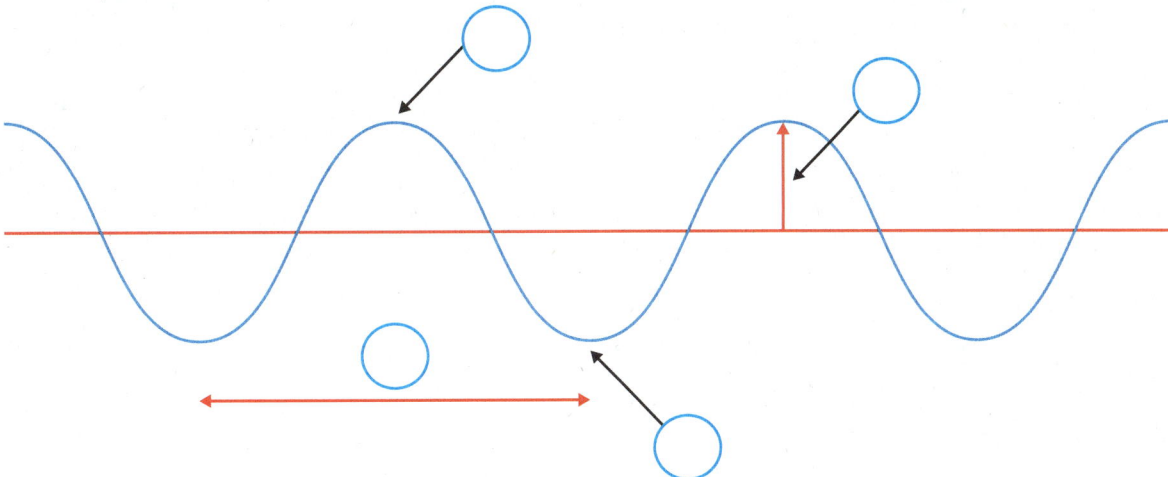

5. Look at the diagram above and observe the pattern of the wave. Find two points on adjacent waves where the distance is the same. Describe these points. Then explain how the crest and trough are connected.

   _____
   _____
   _____
   _____

6. Sound waves can follow varying patterns. Use evidence from this lesson to make a claim about how sound waves have different amounts of energy.

   _____
   _____
   _____
   _____

LESSON 4
Information Transfer

¡Hola!

Salut!

Hello!

Can you hear me?

142 LESSON 4 • Information Transfer

What do you notice about this satellite?

I notice _____

_____

_____

_____

What do you wonder about how information gets from the satellite to Earth?

I wonder _____

_____

_____

_____

Can You Explain It?

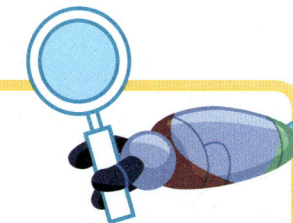

How does a satellite send information to Earth? Sketch, write, or model your answer.

LESSON 4 • Information Transfer

HANDS-ON ACTIVITY

Engineer It
Communication Solution

Have you ever had trouble communicating with someone? Humans communicate in many different ways, and sometimes we have to develop different solutions to communicate. For example, people who are unable to hear can communicate using sign language. In sign language, people use their hands and facial expressions to communicate. People have also found ways to communicate over long distances.

Form a question Ask a question about how to communicate across long distances.

> **Did you know?**
> Around 70 million people in the world use sign language to communicate.

POSSIBLE MATERIALS

☐ cardboard ☐ cups ☐ scissors
☐ cardboard tubes ☐ string
☐ paper ☐ glue

Explore

STEP 1 In the space below, draw a model of a solution that transfers information using patterns.

Make and Test

STEP 2 With your group, make and test your solution using the materials provided. How well did it work? Record your observations below.

LESSON 4 • Information Transfer   145

Improve and Test

STEP 3 How could you improve your solution? Make improvements and test it. Did it work better? Why or why not?

_____

_____

Compare your solution with another group's solution. Record how the solutions are similar and how they are different.

_____

_____

_____

Use **reasoning** to make a **claim** about using patterns to communicate. Cite **evidence** to support your claim.

_____

_____

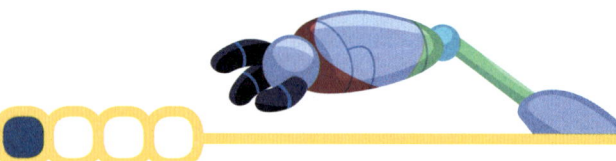

Making Sense

How does your claim and the evidence you gathered from this investigation help you explain how a satellite uses patterns to communicate?

_____

_____

_____

HANDS-ON ACTIVITY

Pixels to Pictures

Have you ever used a magnifying glass to look closely at a picture? If so, you may have seen that the image was made up of millions of tiny dots. Each dot that makes a picture is called a **pixel.** When an image contains many pixels, it will be very sharp. If an image has few pixels, it will be blurry.

Form a question Ask a question about how pixels are used to send information.

_____

_____

_____

> **Did you know?**
>
> The word *pixel* means "picture element."

LESSON 4 • Information Transfer   147

STEP 1 Color in the boxes containing the number 1 to see what the message says.

STEP 2 What does the message say?

_____

0	0	0	0	0	0	0
0	0	0	0	0	0	0
0	1	0	1	0	1	0
0	1	0	1	0	0	0
0	1	0	1	0	1	0
0	1	1	1	0	1	0
0	1	0	1	0	1	0
0	1	0	1	0	1	0
0	1	0	1	0	1	0
0	0	0	0	0	0	0
0	0	0	0	0	0	0

STEP 3 Now you get to decide what message or image to send. Use the ruler to draw a grid on paper. It should have at least ten columns and ten rows.

STEP 4 Fill in each box with the number 1 or 0. Place the 1s in a pattern that will make a message or image.

Communicating well with others is important. Discuss with a partner one way that you think you communicate well.

Each box in the grid represents one pixel. What was the hardest part about making an image using pixels? What was the easiest?

How did you arrange the 1s in your grid used to represent something else?

Use **reasoning** to make a **claim** about pixels. Cite **evidence** to support your claim.

Making Sense

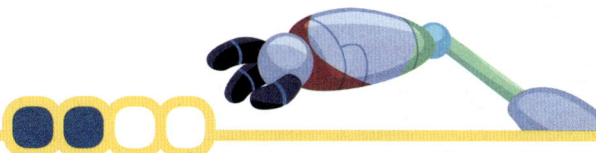

How is using pixels to send messages similar to the way satellites send messages?

LESSON 4 • Information Transfer

EXPLORATION

History of Information Transfer

The Old Ways

Humans always have needed to communicate. As you've discovered, one of the oldest methods of information transfer is information captured by the senses through light and sound. Before people began to talk, they probably sent messages by pointing, grunting, or using signals.

How can people send messages long distances without making any noise? In ancient China, battles often involved soldiers from faraway places. Soldiers used smoke signals to communicate across long distances.

Native Americans on the plains in the Midwest also used smoke to send signals. The smoke signals served as a "universal language" between the tribes.

A talking drum has two heads. It can be tuned to different notes but usually produces low wavelengths. Ancient people used drums to tell stories, send messages, and lead ceremonies. Drums are still important communication tools for cultures of West Africa.

"One if by land. Two if by sea." During Paul Revere's ride to let people know that the British were coming, colonists used lanterns in Boston's Old North Church to send simple messages to many people at once.

Newer Ways

With the discovery of electricity, people could send signals over much greater distances, even thousands of miles. The telegraph, invented in the 1830s, allowed information to travel all over the world along wires. Samuel Morse invented a "language" that could be used to send messages using the telegraph.

International Morse Code

Character	Morse code	Character	Morse code	Number	Morse code
A	·—	N	—·	1	·————
B	—···	O	———	2	··———
C	—·—·	P	·——·	3	···——
D	—··	Q	——·—	4	····—
E	·	R	·—·	5	·····
F	··—·	S	···	6	—····
G	——·	T	—	7	——···
H	····	U	··—	8	———··
I	··	V	···—	9	————·
J	·———	W	·——	0	—————
K	—·—	X	—··—		
L	·—··	Y	—·——		
M	——	Z	——··		

A **code** is a system of letters, numbers, or symbols used in place of words or letters. The telegraph code is called Morse code. It is a series of dots and dashes, each making up a letter. An operator taps out a message. It travels through wires to another location. A second operator decodes the message. When telegraphing was popular, operators had to be skillful so they could send out many messages accurately.

Samuel Morse

LESSON 4 • Information Transfer 151

Telegraphs

People used the telegraph to send messages all over the world. When the telegraph was first invented, cables were laid across the Atlantic Ocean to Europe. During World Wars I and II, the telegraph helped armies keep track of enemies. The last telegraph message was sent in 2013.

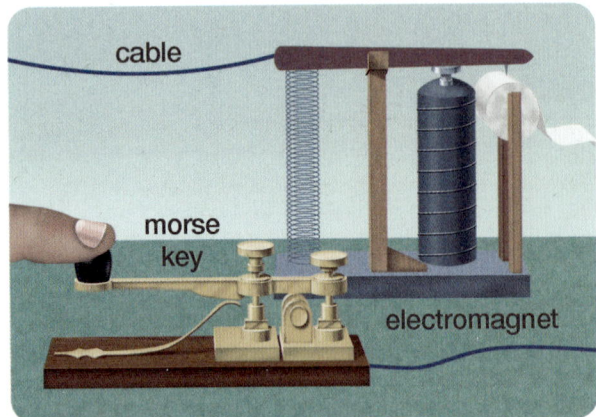

A battery, an electromagnet, a key, and a cable make up a telegraph. By tapping the key, an electric pulse is sent through the cable.

The telegraph operator uses a code called Morse code. It is a series of dots and dashes, each making up a letter.

The signal moves along the cable to a machine on the other end.

The electric pulse is transformed into sound. The operator listens and decodes the dots and dashes to make words from them.

Explain why engineers continue to develop new solutions to communicate with even though the telegraph could send messages over long distances.

Codes

Think about sending a signal. Each message needs a sender and a receiver. You probably talk to or text your friends using a phone or have a face-to-face chat.

How do you make your message clear? Sometimes, text messages don't get the correct message across. If you use shorthand such as symbols or emojis, the receiver may not know what you mean.

Sometimes you might want to send a message that's meant for only one person. Maybe you want to be sure only the receiver can understand the message. You can encode your message and then send it. The receiver will then decode the message.

Flags can relay coded messages, especially between ship and shore or between two people too far away to hear each other.

A **scytale** is another way to send a coded message. In a scytale, a strip is wrapped around a tube. A message is added, and then the tube is removed.

Making Sense

Describe the evidence you found that explains how information can be encoded and transferred. How does this help you understand how a satellite sends information?

_____
_____
_____
_____

LESSON 4 • Information Transfer

EXPLORATION

Bits and Bytes

Bits of Code

In our digital world, everything needs to be changed into code. Pictures, words, and numbers on our devices are converted into codes that can be sent as electronic signals using the numbers 1 and 0. This is called *binary code*. Each number of the code is a *bit*. This is the smallest piece of information that can be stored by a computer. Binary code is a little tricky at first. However, once you get the hang of it, binary code is pretty easy.

Binary code

Connecting the World

Today, a lot of what we do is made easier by wireless technology. We can talk on a cell phone. We can "stream" movies to our TVs or to our handheld devices from wireless Internet modems. We can even listen to music that is relayed as signals from satellites.

All of these things rely on electronic signals transferring bits of code from one place to another. However, these signals can be interrupted. If you have ever had a dropped cell phone call or an Internet video that would not play, you have experienced an interrupted digital code.

The number of bits a device can move or process is a limitation. If a signal has too much information for the network to move, the signal slows down or stops. This is why you hear about the need for high-speed Internet connections.

Today, we listen to music on our phones and other small devices.

154 LESSON 4 • Information Transfer

Code, Computers, and Networks

Humans communicate with words, letters, numbers, and pictures. Computers and other devices do not know what these are. Instead, computers need to translate these forms of communication into code.

Now picture how signals are sent between computers. First, you input words using the keyboard. Then, the computer translates them into binary code. If you are sending an email or a text to a friend, the computer needs to be able to "talk" to the Internet. Computers use a device called a modem to talk to the rest of the world.

Next, the modem sends the signals to and from your computer. When you send an email, the pathway goes from your computer to the modem. It then goes to another modem, then to your friend's computer.

Kesha just sent an email to her grandma. The signal goes from the computer to the modem. It goes across the lines to Grandma's modem and then to her computer.

Grandma is waiting for the email. The signal comes from her modem. The message is transmitted very quickly.

LESSON 4 • Information Transfer

How Computers Help Us Communicate

Electronics are helpful communication tools. When family and friends live far away, computers help us communicate with them quickly. Being able to communicate with people far away keeps people connected.

When you write an email, your computer encodes your words.

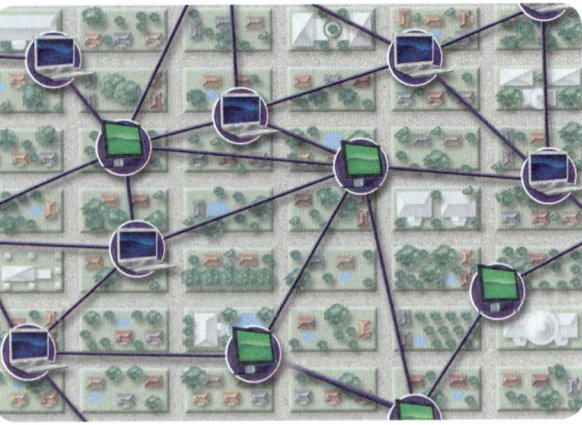

The codes are first sent through your local area network, or LAN, which is made up of all the modems in a virtual neighborhood.

The LAN sends the signals to all the computers that make up the Internet.

The signals containing coded words and pictures are decoded by the receiver. Your message can now be read.

 Share with your neighbors about how technology has helped you communicate better.

156 LESSON 4 • Information Transfer

How Cell Phones Help Us Communicate

Cell phones help us communicate faster and more efficiently. We can call and talk to someone or send a text message. Being able to communicate when we need to is a big advantage in emergencies.

When you talk on a cell phone, the sound waves of your voice are converted into digital code. The code is then sent as radio waves through the air.

The sender's radio waves reach cell phone towers, which exist in a network around the entire world.

The waves are relayed from tower to tower to satellites and then to other towers.

The radio waves are received by a cell phone, which converts them back into sound.

Bits of Color

Pixels are important. Remember that each picture or image you see on a screen is made of pixels. The more pixels there are, the clearer and crisper the image will be. Back in the 1980s, video games and TVs had a lower resolution than they do today. This means there were fewer pixels on the screen. Today's screens feature many more pixels, making the pictures much clearer and the colors brighter. This is called high resolution, or high definition. You might have heard it called HD.

Does this image look like an apple? The image has very low resolution, meaning it contains very few pixels. The edges look fuzzy. The texture looks grainy. This is how television and computer pictures looked many years ago.

Here is an image with slightly higher resolution. Notice how much clearer it is. The image also looks much smoother and more realistic. Most people today like to see higher-resolution images. They look more realistic than low-resolution images.

Making Sense

How does your understanding of how we use technology to communicate help you understand how a satellite sends digitized information?

Name _____

Lesson Check

Can You Explain It?

Review your ideas from the beginning of this lesson about how information is transferred. How have your ideas changed?

Be sure to do the following:

- Describe how patterns are used to send messages.
- Explain how information is encoded, moved long distances, and then decoded without losing any of the information.

Now I know or think that _____

_____

_____

_____

Making Connections

Nowadays, people can use their mobile devices to make video calls to friends and family members. How is this similar to a satellite?

_____

_____

_____

_____

LESSON 4 • Information Transfer   159

Checkpoints

1. Suppose you want to describe African drums to a classmate. You want to explain how people use drums to send each other signals using patterns. Which of these would you say? Circle all that apply.

   a. The drums send signals you can hear.
   b. The drums have a very high wavelength.
   c. The drums have a very low wavelength.
   d. Different drumming patterns mean different things.

2. Telegraph operators used electric pulses to create patterns. The patterns were then decoded to create messages. The messages were not always reliable. Name some ways a message might be miscommunicated or misunderstood, and explain your reasoning.

   _____

   _____

3. Put these steps in order to explain how a message gets from your cell phone to your friend's cell phone.

   [tower near your friend's cell phone]   [tower close to your cell phone]   [friend's cell phone]

   [your cell phone]   [relay]

4. Use the code key pattern below to decode the message. (Hint: it is six words long.) The message is:
   9 12 5 1 18 14 5 4 13 1 14 25 20 8 9 14 7 19 1 2 15
   21 20 19 9 7 14 1 12 19

1	2	3	4	5	6	7	8	9	10	11	12	13
A	B	C	D	E	F	G	H	I	J	K	L	M
14	15	16	17	18	19	20	21	22	23	24	25	26
N	O	P	Q	R	S	T	U	V	W	X	Y	Z

5. Which of these methods use technology, patterns, or both to transmit information? Circle all that apply.
   a. Morse code
   b. flags
   c. scytale
   d. texts to a friend using your phone

6. Cell phones use patterns to encode messages. How are cell phone signals transferred? Circle the best answer.
   a. They go from the tower to the phone, then to another phone.
   b. They go from the receiver's phone to the sender's phone.
   c. They go from sender to tower, to relay, to tower, then to receiver.
   d. They go from tower to receiver, to sender, to relay, then back to the receiver.

7. Some communication methods use coded communication. Others use uncoded communication. Draw a line from each method to the type of communication it uses. Some may use both types.

coded	Morse code	uncoded
	talking on the phone	
	scytale	
	text message	
	talking face to face	

8. Many communication methods use codes. Why are codes a useful way to relay messages? Circle all that apply.
   a. They do not depend on understanding a language.
   b. Everyone can understand them.
   c. They can be encoded and decoded digitally and sent by waves.
   d. They are short.

Name _____

Unit Review

1. Which kind of energy is being demonstrated in this image?

   a. motion
   b. spring
   c. wind
   d. heat

2. What happens to a cue ball when it collides with another ball? Circle all that apply.

   a. It changes direction.
   b. It gains stored energy.
   c. It gains energy of motion.
   d. It loses some of its energy.

3. A local cell phone company built a tower near an airport. The tower is difficult to see at night. How can you use what you know about the transfer of energy to help prevent planes from hitting the new tower. What are two criteria and one constraint you must consider in your solution?

   _____
   _____
   _____
   _____

4. Which statement below best describes a system of energy transformation shown in the image? Circle the correct choice.

   a. electrical energy into light and heat
   b. sound and motion into light and heat
   c. light and heat into sound and motion
   d. electrical energy into sound and motion

162 UNIT 3 • Energy and Communication

5. Heat is a form of energy. Explain how the flame, bowl and water create a system that transfers energy. Use evidence to support your answer.

_____

_____

_____

_____

_____

6. What two types of waves are produced by this band performance? Circle the correct choices.

  a. light waves
  b. water waves
  c. sound waves
  d. seismic waves

7. When you play mini golf, sometimes you have to make the ball go a short distance, and sometimes you need to make it go a long distance. Use this example to explain the relationship between speed and energy.

_____

_____

_____

_____

_____

8. In an ocean wave, what is moving toward the shore—the water or the energy? What evidence do you have to support your answer?

_____

_____

_____

_____

9. Elephants use low-frequency sounds to communicate across very long distances. How is this similar to the way we use cell phones? How is it different?

_____

_____

_____

_____

10. How did the ancient Chinese use patterns as a solution to the problem of communicating over long distances?

_____

_____

_____

_____

In Unit 3, you used models of waves to discover patterns in the motion of waves and how waves cause changes. In this unit, you will use evidence from patterns in rock to explain how landscapes change over time.

UNIT 4 Shaping Landforms

Lesson 1
Factors That Shape Earth's Surface............ 166

Lesson 2
Fast and Slow Changes 182

Lesson 3
Rock Layers Record Landform Changes..... 198

Unit 4 Review.. 218

LESSON 1

Factors That Shape Earth's Surface

What a view!

What do you notice about the canyon?

I notice _____

_____

_____

_____

_____

What do you wonder about how the canyon formed?

I wonder _____

_____

_____

_____

_____

Can You Explain It?

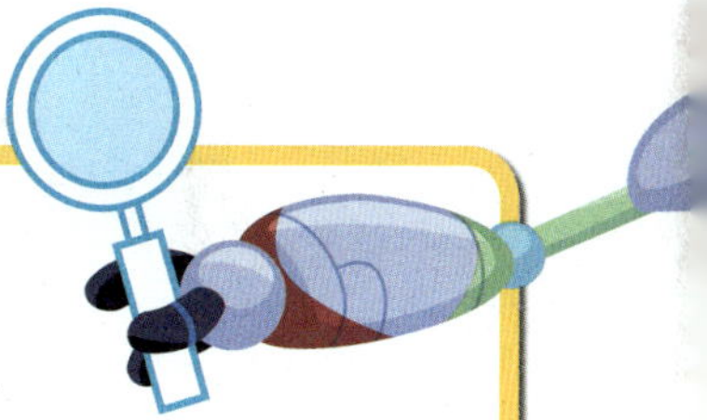

How did the canyon form in the middle of flat land? Sketch, write, or model your answer.

LESSON 1 • Factors That Shape Earth's Surface

HANDS-ON ACTIVITY

Modeling How Far Sediment Travels

Many factors affect how landforms change. Wind can change the way landforms look, and it also can move sediment, which is made up of soil and small pieces of rock, from place to place. Observe the sand dunes in the image. The shape of a sand dune constantly changes.

Form a question Ask a question about how wind can affect the motion of soil and small pieces of rock.

Did you know?
All dunes have two parts: the slip face and the windward side. The slip face is the side away from the wind. The windward side is the side facing the oncoming wind.

_____
_____
_____
_____

POSSIBLE MATERIALS

- [ ] fan
- [ ] butcher paper, 1.5 m per team
- [ ] masking tape
- [ ] beaker of silt, 200 mL
- [ ] sand
- [ ] gravel
- [ ] meterstick
- [ ] stopwatch
- [ ] safety goggles

STEP 1 **Investigate your question** How can you use a model to investigate the question you asked? Think about the materials your teacher shows you, and consider what else you might need. Write your investigation plan below. If you want to use materials other than those your teacher shows you, be sure to write them in the plan. Then, show your teacher the plan to see if you can get the additional materials you need.

_____
_____
_____
_____

STEP 2 Carry out your plan, and record your results on a separate sheet of paper. Observe evidence of change.

LESSON 1 • Factors That Shape Earth's Surface   169

STEP 3 Present your data so everyone can see what you did and understand what happened. You may wish to use a table or graph as a presentation tool or show your findings in a poster.

Make a **claim** about how wind moves sediment. Support your claim with **evidence** from your investigation, and explain with **reasoning**.

_____
_____
_____
_____

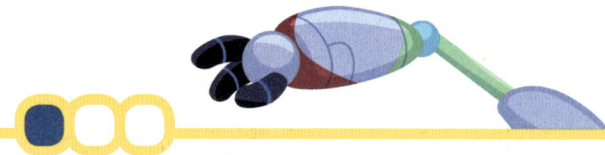

Making Sense

How does your understanding of how far sediment travels by wind help you understand how the canyon was formed?

_____
_____
_____
_____
_____

Public speaking can be scary for some people. Talk with your group about strategies for calming down before a presentation. Choose one to try out, and then share how well it works.

LESSON 1 • Factors That Shape Earth's Surface

HANDS-ON ACTIVITY

A Sweet Test

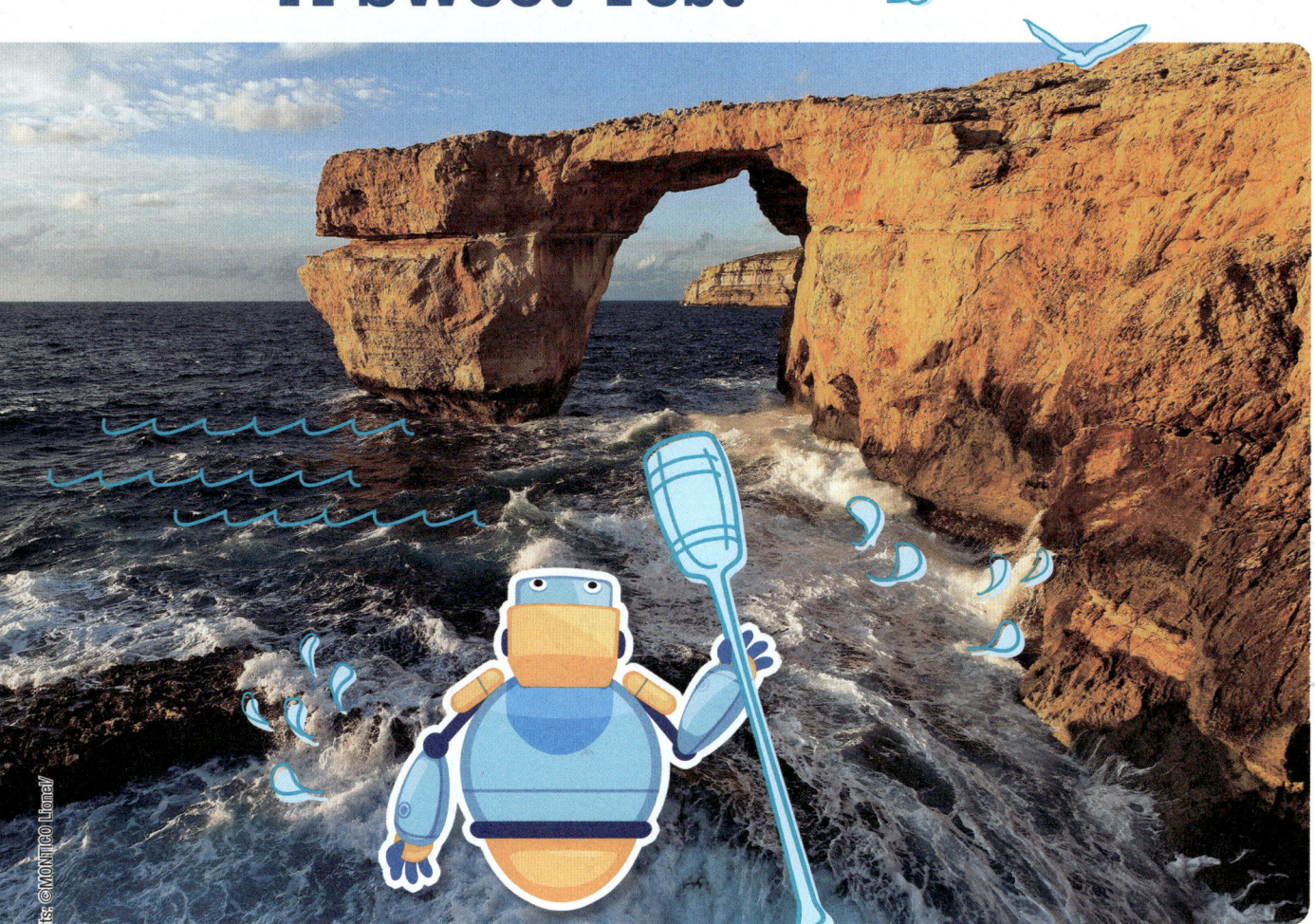

All landforms change over time. Even the slightest change to Earth processes can cause landforms to grow bigger, break apart, or smooth over. Moving water can cause landforms to change.

Form a question Ask a question about how water can cause changes to Earth's surface.

> **Did you know?**
> The roof of a sea arch is known as the keystone.

LESSON 1 • Factors That Shape Earth's Surface

POSSIBLE MATERIALS
- [ ] small, lidded container
- [ ] sugar cubes, 2
- [ ] water
- [ ] pipette

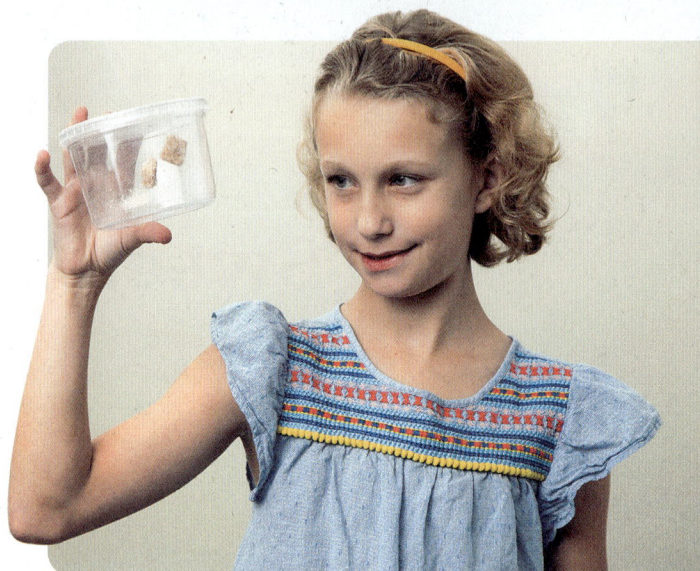

STEP 1 Put a sugar cube inside the container and put the lid on. Shake the container for 30 seconds. Open the lid and make observations.

_____

_____

STEP 2 Empty the container, and place a new sugar cube inside. Use the pipette to put three drops of water in the container, and then put the lid on. Shake the container for 30 seconds. Open the lid and make observations.

_____

_____

Make a **claim** about how water affects the rate at which Earth's surface changes. Use **evidence** from your investigation and explain your **reasoning.**

_____

_____

Making Sense

How did modeling how water can change Earth's surface help you better understand how the river helped form the canyon?

_____

_____

_____

EXPLORATION

Earth's Surface

Changes You Can See

Forces on Earth's surface constantly change, sculpt, and reshape rocks. Small changes might happen near you. Big ones might occur, too.

Have you ever noticed sediment and debris washed onto the sidewalk after it rains? This is an example of a local, or small-scale, change caused by Earth's surface processes.

Some of the processes that change the way the sidewalk looks after rainfall also changed the Sierra Nevada Mountains. Ice, wind, and running water have shaped these mountains.

Earth's Changing Surface

Many processes constantly change Earth's surface.

Weathering is the breaking down of rocks on Earth's surface into smaller pieces. Weathering occurs in rivers when the current causes rocks to bump against one another and break apart.

Erosion is the movement of weathered rock and soil from one place to another. Rivers create erosion when they move rock and soil downstream. Wind, gravity, and other forces also can cause erosion.

Deposition occurs when water slows downs and drops the rocks and sediment it carries. This occurs at the mouths of rivers and anywhere else water slows down or stops moving. The wind can cause deposition, too. Sand dunes result from wind deposition.

Water Weathering

Water is the main cause of weathering and erosion. Rivers change the areas they flow through. Flooding can move sediment. Waves can crumble cliffs.

Many factors affect the rates of weathering, erosion, and deposition. The amount of water, the angle of a slope, and the rate of deposition can all affect how slowly or quickly these processes occur.

Rainfall shapes the land. When a lot of rain falls, it flows in many directions, quickly washing away materials and moving soil to different places.

Strong currents, such as those of California's Kern River, can slowly erode landforms by crashing into rocks.

Moving water in Colca Canyon in Peru slowly weathered and eroded parts of the land, carving into Earth's surface.

Moving Water!

Rain, rivers, oceans, and other moving water can gradually change Earth's surface by wearing it away. Moving water carries away sediment. Over millions of years, rivers can carve mile-deep canyons by weathering and eroding rock, sending sediment downstream. Moving water can also change the path of a river.

Sandy beaches form when waves break pebbles into smaller pieces. Ocean waves also weather rock and can move sand from one beach to another. Observe the images above. Circle evidence of change taking place in each image.

Cold as Ice

Liquid water turns to ice when the temperature is at or below 0 °C (32 °F). Ice becomes liquid water again when the ice thaws, or melts. This cycle of freezing and thawing happens constantly. Can this pattern cause weathering and erosion? Examine the images to see how ice affects rocks.

① There is a small crack in the surface of this rock.

② The crack fills with rain or melting snow.

③ If the temperature is cold enough, the water turns to ice. Water expands when it freezes.

④ When the temperature rises above 0 °C, the ice melts. Compare the crack now to the original one.

⑤ The crack is wider. When the pattern repeats many times, rock pieces may break off, weather, and be carried away, or erode.

Predict Draw and label what might happen next to the rock and ice. Write a caption.

LESSON 1 • Factors That Shape Earth's Surface

Windy Forces

Wind may also cause weathering, erosion, and deposition. Over time, sand weathers rock by breaking it into smaller pieces. The weathered pieces of rock are carried by the wind. When the wind slows down, the pieces come to rest in a new location.

Winds can change the way landforms look. California's Jacumba Wind Caves were weathered by winds over a long period of time.

Sand dunes are the result of wind deposition. The wind leaves small piles of sand. Slowly, sand builds up, and sand dunes are formed.

Paria Canyon, in Utah and Arizona, shows off unique patterns that were carved into rock by the wind over time.

Find an example of weathering by wind in your state. Draw a picture of your example, and write a caption for it.

Identify Which of the following is an example of erosion?

a. water sitting at the bottom of a pond
b. sunlight shining on a mountain
c. rain falling over a lake
d. wind blowing away sediment

Water World

Water can change Earth's surface in direct ways, such as the sea eroding a sandy beach or a river carving a canyon into the land. But water can also allow living things to live, grow, and thrive in their environment. An **environment** is all the living and nonliving things that surround and affect an organism.

Deserts get less than 26 cm (10 in.) of precipitation each year. Living things need water to survive and grow. Deserts' dry conditions limit the number of species in this environment.

Rainforests get at least 203 cm (80 in.) of precipitation each year. Many different plant and animal species can survive here.

Living Things Change Their Environments

A soccer or football field may have patches of dirt where players' cleats wore away the grass. Similarly, a walking trail through the woods may be rockier and more worn down than the area surrounding it.

Animals, plants, and other organisms can have similar effects on Earth's surface. Look at the images to see how organisms affect their environment.

As the roots of plants grow, they widen the cracks in rocks, sometimes making rocks split or fall away.

Meerkats live in burrows. As they dig, they move dirt to Earth's surface. This dirt may be carried away by wind or rain water, or it may mix with dirt on the surface.

LESSON 1 • Factors That Shape Earth's Surface   177

Ivy is a type of plant that grows up and around other objects. As ivy climbs, it sends out small roots that change their shape to cling to the surface the ivy is climbing. These roots can push into cracks in rock.

Organism Cause and Effect

You've looked at how organisms can be forces of erosion, weathering, and deposition. Just like water, animals, plants, and other living organisms can change the physical features of Earth's surface. Many times, these changes enable organisms to survive within their environment. Study each image and caption, and write the effect caused by each change.

Beavers are dam builders. By toppling trees across streams, they cause the level of water behind the dam to rise.

This type of termite builds large mounds out of soil. When the mound erodes due to wind or rain, the termites replace it with fresh soil.

Making Sense

You've explored the effects wind and water have on Earth's surface. How do your findings help you understand how the canyon was formed?

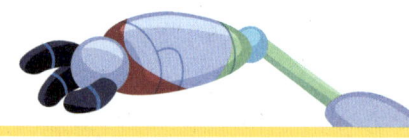

178 LESSON 1 • Factors That Shape Earth's Surface

Name _____

Lesson Check

Can You Explain It?

Now that you've learned about factors that shape Earth's surface, explain how you think this canyon formed over time. Be sure to do the following:

- Explain how the river changed the canyon over time.
- Describe how weathering and erosion changed the canyon.
- Describe how plants, animals, and other organisms could have helped change parts of the canyon.

Now I know or think that _____

_____

_____

Making Connections

A rock bridge, like the one shown here, has this shape because moving water broke off pieces of rock and eventually created a hole in the rock. How is this rock bridge similar to the canyon from the beginning of the lesson? How is it different?

_____

_____

_____

_____

LESSON 1 • Factors That Shape Earth's Surface

Checkpoints

1. Which statement best explains what causes sand dunes to form?
    a. They are the result of wind deposition.
    b. They are created by water currents.
    c. They are created by water erosion.
    d. They are the result of water weathering.

2. Which is an example of the effects of erosion?
    a. Ocean waves move sand from one beach to another.
    b. Plant roots break rock beneath the surface of Earth.
    c. Tree roots break parts of a sidewalk.
    d. Heavy blocks of ice crack rocks to form caves.

3. Give an example of evidence showing that animals play a role in how landforms change.

_____

_____

_____

_____

4. Describe how water is a factor in a pattern that causes changes to Earth's surface.

_____

_____

_____

5. Which of the following is not evidence of deposition?
   a. Damp sediment is piled up at the base of a mountain after the snow has melted.
   b. A river is wider and its water is dirtier after a flash flood has occurred upriver.
   c. A hiker finds small, flat rocks stacked at the peak of a mountain.
   d. A beach appears to have more sand after a large ocean storm.

6. How can water, ice, wind, and plants cause weathering in land structures? Provide an example for each.

_____
_____
_____
_____
_____

7. What might scientists do to observe the effects of erosion?
   a. measure the height of a mountain, and monitor the height over time
   b. study the temperature at which water freezes into ice
   c. predict how large plant roots will grow
   d. follow weather patterns to see when it will be dry and hot

8. Which statement accurately describes how wind can affect land features?
   a. It can cause rocks to freeze and break.
   b. It can erode loose pieces of sand.
   c. It can make immediate changes to rock.
   d. It can change the direction water flows to prevent erosion.

LESSON 1 • Factors That Shape Earth's Surface

LESSON 2
Fast and Slow Changes

Glad I brought my umbrella hat!

What do you notice about the flooded area? What do you notice about the canyon?

I notice _____

_____

_____

_____

What do you wonder about how Earth has changed over time?

I wonder _____

_____

_____

_____

Can You Explain It?

What affects the speed at which Earth's surface changes? Sketch, write, or model your answer.

LESSON 2 • **Fast and Slow Changes**

HANDS-ON ACTIVITY

The Rate of Change

Earth's surface changes constantly as forces reshape rocks. Sometimes these forces act quickly, and at other times they cause changes more slowly. The slope, or angle of incline or decline, of the land can also affect how quickly Earth's surface changes.

Form a question Ask a question about how slope affects changes in Earth's surface.

Did you know?
Landslides can move at speeds of around 80 km/h (50 mph).

_____
_____
_____
_____

POSSIBLE MATERIALS

- [ ] paper cup
- [ ] sharpened pencil
- [ ] plastic drinking straw
- [ ] scissors
- [ ] small piece of modeling clay
- [ ] piece of cardboard, 31-cm square
- [ ] soil
- [ ] ruler
- [ ] large bottle filled with water (approx. 2L)

STEP 1 **Investigate your question** Many factors affect soil erosion on a slope. In the space below, plan an investigation that models how slope affects the rate of erosion.

STEP 2 **Carry out your plan** As you conduct your investigation, record your observations and data on the next page.

Neat!

LESSON 2 • Fast and Slow Changes

STEP 3 Record your data in the space below.

STEP 4 Describe what happens to the soil when the slope changes.

___
___
___
___

STEP 5 **Draw conclusions** Share your conclusions with another group. What similarities and differences do you notice?

Make a **claim** about how the slope of Earth's surface affects the rate of erosion. Support your claim with **evidence** from your investigation, and explain your **reasoning**.

When you work with others, everyone may have different ideas. What are some strategies that help you make sure everyone can share their thoughts?

Making Sense

How does understanding how slope affects erosion help you explain the speed at which Earth's surface changes?

LESSON 2 • Fast and Slow Changes

HANDS-ON ACTIVITY

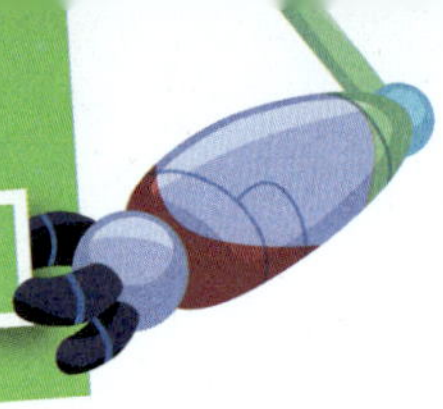

Glaciers on the Move

In some areas of the world, the environment is cold enough for huge sheets of ice to form and stay frozen all year round. These large ice sheets are called glaciers. Glaciers flow like very slow-moving rivers of ice. Imagine what might happen to the land underneath a large glacier.

Form a question What question do you have about glaciers?

_____
_____
_____
_____

Did you know?

One of the largest glaciers on Earth is about 97 km (60 mi) wide and 435 km (270 mi) long.

POSSIBLE MATERIALS
- [ ] ice in plastic cup
- [ ] spoonful of sand
- [ ] spoonful of gravel
- [ ] spoonful of dirt
- [ ] water
- [ ] piece of cardboard
- [ ] large ball of clay
- [ ] wooden block

STEP 1 **Investigate your question** Flatten the clay to cover the piece of cardboard and then sprinkle sand on top. Place the wooden block under one end of the cardboard to create a slope. Remove the piece of ice from the cup, and place it on the higher end of the cardboard. Using one hand, slowly push your "glacier" down the incline.

STEP 2 Record your observations on a separate sheet of paper. Repeat the process twice more, recording your observations.

Identify the **evidence** that supports your **claim** about the factors that affect the rate in which Earth's surface changes. Explain your **reasoning**.

_____
_____
_____

Making Sense

How does understanding how glaciers change Earth's surface help you understand the factors that affect the rate of change on Earth's surface?

_____
_____
_____

LESSON 2 • Fast and Slow Changes

EXPLORATION

Fast Changes

The surface of Earth changes constantly. New mountains, rivers, and lakes form, and old ones disappear. Many of these changes happen slowly. However, powerful forces can cause landforms to change very quickly.

Landslides occur when part of the land breaks apart and falls. Mudslides occur when the land becomes soaked with water and the muddy earth and debris fall.

Volcanic eruptions can cause fast or slow changes to Earth. When volcanoes erupt, lava and other debris can destroy parts of the land very quickly. Volcanic eruptions also can slowly create new landforms.

Earthquakes happen suddenly and can cause change very quickly. The force of an earthquake can break rocks and tear apart the ground.

These quick changes can have major impacts. Often, people have to assess the damage and develop solutions to help restore Earth's surface. Sometimes, however, the changes can be positive, creating new land or supplying water and nutrients to the environment.

Hurricanes are tropical storms that bring heavy winds and rains. They occur quickly and can uproot trees and damage human structures.

Floods are overflows of water. Floods are powerful and can move quickly over or through anything in their paths. Like hurricanes, floods can destroy natural and human structures.

Analyze Which of the following is an example of a fast change to Earth's surface?

a. a volcano creating a new island in the ocean

b. a river that flows through a canyon

c. an earthquake that breaks apart the ground

d. a windy day that makes small trees and plants shake

Making Sense

Describe the evidence you found to support your claim about how fast Earth's surface changes.

LESSON 2 • Fast and Slow Changes

EXPLORATION

Slow Changes

Slow and Steady

Some events quickly cause changes to Earth's surface. Other events cause changes that occur much more slowly. Different factors affect the speed of change to Earth's surface, such as the rate of erosion.

A slow-moving river can weather land structures and cause erosion and deposition. A slow-moving river doesn't cause structural change as rapidly as a fast-flowing river because it does not have as much force. But both fast and slow-moving rivers take years to change the landscape.

Plants can squeeze their way through the soil and slowly wedge pieces of the ground apart. These pieces don't move very far. The amount of rainfall can affect how fast plant roots grow.

Pushing Through

A glacier is a river of ice moving downhill, usually very slowly. Glaciers are found in the cold polar zones or cold, high mountain valleys. Glaciers weather the rock beneath them. They scrape and cut rock as they slide over the ground. Glaciers also cause erosion by pushing broken pieces of rock under and on top of them as they move. Deposition occurs when glaciers melt and leave behind the rocks they carried.

As this glacier moves, it pushes rocks along with it.

Glaciers change the land they flow through.

As the ice melts, glaciers also leave sediment behind.

Water Processes

Weathering, erosion, and deposition happen at different speeds. The speed of change can be affected by the amount of water, the angle of a slope, and rate of deposition, among other forces.

Changing the Shape of Land

Look at the images, and then label each one with the letter corresponding to the correct description below.

a. Heavy rain can cause mudslides. When the ground is steep, water and mud slide down faster due to the force of gravity. This causes more erosion.

b. Waves cause weathering and erosion on rocky beaches. The force of the pounding waves splits and chips rock. Then, the water carries the rock pieces away.

c. A swiftly flowing stream carries sediment and rocks downstream, causing erosion.

d. Falling water weathers the stone under it. Erosion causes pieces of rock to drop away. Then, deposition piles the rocks up under the falling water.

 What are some strategies you can use to complete the activity above if you are unsure of the answers? Discuss some of your strategies with a classmate.

LESSON 2 • Fast and Slow Changes

Sand and Time

The images on this page show how wind makes slow changes to landforms over time. Think about how climate can affect how fast or slow wind causes weathering, erosion, and deposition.

Study the pictures closely. Choose the factor involved in each example.

1. Wind transports sand across the landscape. Some of this sand comes into contact with parts of a large boulder. Over time, the boulder is worn away.
   a. Wind deposits the boulder.
   b. Wind-blown sand weathers the lower part of the boulder.
   c. Moving water erodes the lower part of the boulder.

2. Wind transports sand and other types of sediment from the base of a hill.
   a. Wind erodes on the lower part of the slope.
   b. Sand is deposited at the top of the slope.
   c. Moving water erodes the base of the hill.

3. As wind transports sand across a landscape, the sand can build up in certain areas.
   a. Sand is deposited.
   b. Sand is weathered.
   c. Moving water deposits sand and erodes dunes.

Making Sense

Use images in this lesson to explain the factors that affect how quickly Earth's surface changes.

Name _____

Lesson Check

Can You Explain It?

Now that you've learned more about other factors that shape Earth's surface, explain what affects the speed at which Earth's surface changes. Be sure to do the following:

- Explain what forces shaped Earth's surface and whether they happened quickly or slowly.
- Use the terms *erosion* and *weathering* in your answer.

Now I know or think that _____

_____

_____

_____

_____

Making Connections

Moving water can cause Earth's surface to change both quickly and slowly. How is this waterfall like the flooded area and the canyon formed by the river?

_____

_____

_____

LESSON 2 • Fast and Slow Changes   195

Checkpoints

1. Which statement below is evidence of gravity's effect on Earth's surface?
   a. Plant roots push up and out of the soil.
   b. Cracks along the ground develop over long periods.
   c. Rocks, water, and mud fall from higher to lower points.
   d. Digging animals can't burrow very deep into the ground.

2. Which process shaped the sand dunes in this photo of a desert area?
   a. Sand was deposited by wind.
   b. Glaciers carried sand to this new location.
   c. Gravity forces the piles up higher.
   d. Sand is being weathered by water.

3. What forces likely caused the changes shown in the photo of a rocky hillside? Use evidence to support your claim.

_____
_____
_____
_____
_____

4. Which force of nature shaped the landform shown in the image?
   a. flood
   b. landslide
   c. glacier
   d. waves

   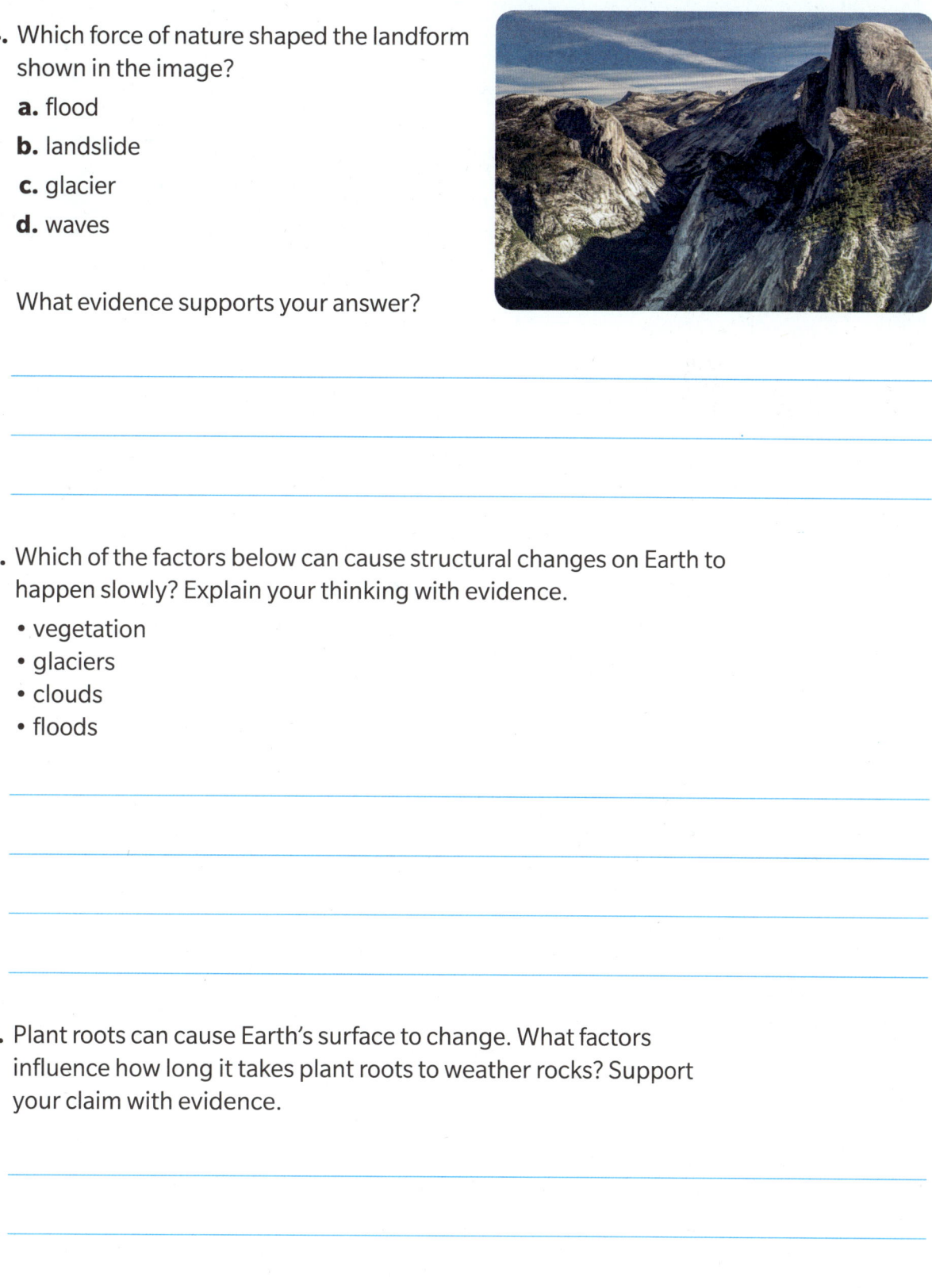

   What evidence supports your answer?

   _____
   _____
   _____

5. Which of the factors below can cause structural changes on Earth to happen slowly? Explain your thinking with evidence.
   • vegetation
   • glaciers
   • clouds
   • floods

   _____
   _____
   _____
   _____

6. Plant roots can cause Earth's surface to change. What factors influence how long it takes plant roots to weather rocks? Support your claim with evidence.

   _____
   _____
   _____
   _____

LESSON 2 • Fast and Slow Changes

LESSON 3
Rock Layers Record Landform Changes

Whoa! What are those things?

What do you notice about this rock wall?

I notice _____
_____
_____
_____

What do you wonder about the prints on the wall?

I wonder _____
_____
_____
_____

Can You Explain It?

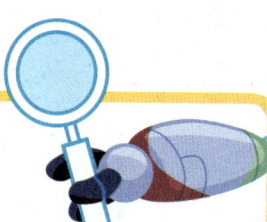

What can you tell about the past environment by studying this rock wall? Sketch, write, or model your answer.

LESSON 3 • Rock Layers Record Landform Changes

HANDS-ON ACTIVITY

Layered Landforms

Rocks can give clues about things that happened on Earth a long time ago. They provide evidence of how the surface of our planet has changed over time. Some rocks formed in ancient oceans. Other rocks formed on dry land.

Form a question Ask a question about rock layers.

Did you know?
Layers of sedimentary rocks are called *strata*.

POSSIBLE MATERIALS
- [ ] large, clear container
- [ ] smaller containers of sand of different colors

STEP 1 With your group, select one sand color. This sand will be the first layer in your jar.

STEP 2 Slowly pour the sand into the jar at a steady rate for 4 seconds.

STEP 3 Repeat the process three more times, changing the sand color and the length of time you pour. Pour one time for 7 seconds, the next time for 13 seconds, and the final time for 10 seconds. Always pour at a steady rate.

Draw conclusions Which layer of sand in your model is the oldest? Which is the youngest? How did pouring the material for longer or shorter periods affect the layers? Use **evidence** and **reasoning** to support your **claims**.

Making Sense

How does modeling rock layers help you better understand how the prints got on the rock wall?

LESSON 3 • Rock Layers Record Landform Changes

HANDS-ON ACTIVITY

Layer by Layer

Scientists can tell the relative age of rocks by looking at where they fall in a sequence. **Relative age** is the age of one thing compared to another. Relative age explains things in terms of older and younger. Landforms often are made of many rock layers. The layers can provide clues about how a part of Earth changed over time.

Form a question Ask a question about how different environments change over time.

> **Did you know?**
> Some rocks are millions of years old.

POSSIBLE MATERIALS
- [ ] nature magazines
- [ ] scissors
- [ ] construction paper
- [ ] glue

STEP 1 Your teacher will provide you with magazines or other sources of photos of present-day environments. Study the photos and discuss with your group what type of environment each one shows. Share evidence for your ideas.

STEP 2 Find images of three different organisms from the same environment, and use scissors to cut each one out so that you cannot see the environment. Each group member should choose three different organisms.

STEP 3 Paste your three organisms randomly on one piece of construction paper. Have your group members do the same, each pasting three organisms onto a piece of paper.

 Someone may take a little longer than others to complete a task, and the rest of the group may be kept waiting. How can you help out that person so that no one gets frustrated?

_____
_____
_____

LESSON 3 • Rock Layers Record Landform Changes

STEP 4 After everyone in your group has glued their organisms onto their papers, stack all the pieces of paper face down in the middle of the table.

STEP 5 Flip the stack over. Your teacher will provide you with the top layer. Trade your layers with another group.

STEP 6 Look at each layer of your new stack. Talk about each organism. Discuss what type of environment the organism would live in and how you know.

STEP 7 Talk with other members of your group about which environment came first and which came later.

STEP 8 List the environments in the chart below, layer by layer, from oldest to youngest. Include observations that helped you identify the environments. You may not need all the rows.

Relative age	Observations	Type of environment
1st environment		
2nd environment		
3rd environment		
4th environment		
5th environment		

By only showing a few organisms in the environment without describing where they live, what do you think you modeled?

_____
_____
_____

Draw conclusions Based on where each layer is in the stack, which environment came first in this area? Which is the newest environment?

_____
_____
_____

Make a **claim** about fossils and environments. Cite **evidence** and explain your **reasoning**.

_____
_____
_____
_____
_____

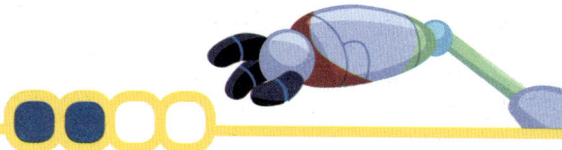

Making Sense

How does the evidence from this investigation help you understand how the footprints were made on the vertical rock wall?

_____
_____
_____

EXPLORATION

Layers of Rock

The photos show rocks in different parts of the world. Study the images to construct an explanation for patterns that you observe in these rocks.

Akaroa Head is in New Zealand, an island country located near Australia. The ocean has shaped this landform.

The Alps are a mountain range that stretches across Europe. Ice and water have slowly shaped the Alps.

Cabrillo National Monument is in San Diego, California. Layers of rock have been washed away by ocean waves over a long period.

Colorful rock layers surround this waterfall near Stoney Creek, in the Canadian province of Ontario.

Scientists can usually tell the relative age of rock layers, or their age compared to other layers, by looking at their order in sequence.

A Long, Long Story!

Use a thin highlighter or a pen to trace the tops and bottoms of as many layers as you can in this photo of a rock formation found in Utah's Capitol Reef National Park. Then, number the layers, marking the oldest layer as 1.

Infer Where in the image is the oldest layer of rock found?

Explain What can the thickness of the rock layers tell you?

There are patterns in the colors of the rocks. What might these patterns mean?

When one rock layer differs from another, this shows that the layers formed in different ways. For example, layers may contain different materials, which means the environment was different when each layer formed. Thinner and thicker layers also suggest conditions differed when the layers formed. Thicker layers may have formed over longer periods when environmental conditions remained stable.

Making Sense

Describe the evidence that supports your claim about rocky layers and how the footprints were made on a vertical rock wall.

LESSON 3 • Rock Layers Record Landform Changes

EXPLORATION

Evidence of Environments

Fossils and Environments

Your backyard might once have been under a sea! Fossils in your area can tell you whether that was the case. **Fossils** are the preserved remains or traces of an organism. Read the descriptions of the fossils shown below. Then, write whether the organism lived in a land or water environment.

Ammonites are extinct animals that lived in coiled shells. They moved by squirting jets of water from their bodies.

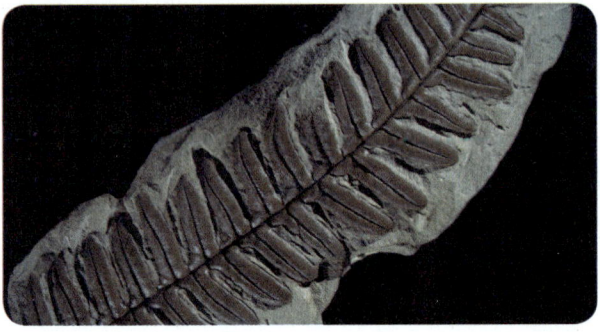

Ferns are plants that live in warm, moist environments such as rainforests. This fossil is an imprint of a fern leaf.

Fish use their fins and tails to move. They often live and move together in large groups, or schools.

Snails are small animals that live in coiled shells. They slide slowly along surfaces with a flat foot made of muscle.

Fossils provide clues about the environments in which the organisms lived, when they lived, and how the environment changed over time. Fossils such as fish and ammonites indicate an aquatic environment. Fossils of certain plants may indicate a terrestrial, or land, environment.

Seeing History

Many locations around the world are rich with fossils. Some of these places have rock layers containing fossils from various types of organisms. All the fossils below were found in one of these locations.

Identify Look at the fossils. On each image, write the letter that corresponds to each fossil's description.

a. This fossil is a snake. You can see its backbone, skull, and ribs.
b. Small fossil shrimp are common in this area. This is one example.
c. The leaf of a plant clearly shows in this fossil. It is the leaf of a willow tree. Plants give scientists important clues to past environments.
d. Some rock layers here are full of fish fossils. Consider the types of environments in which fish were common.

Building the Story

Analyze Look at the images of rock layers and the fossils found in them. For each fossil in the chart below, identify the type of environment the organism lived in (either land or water).

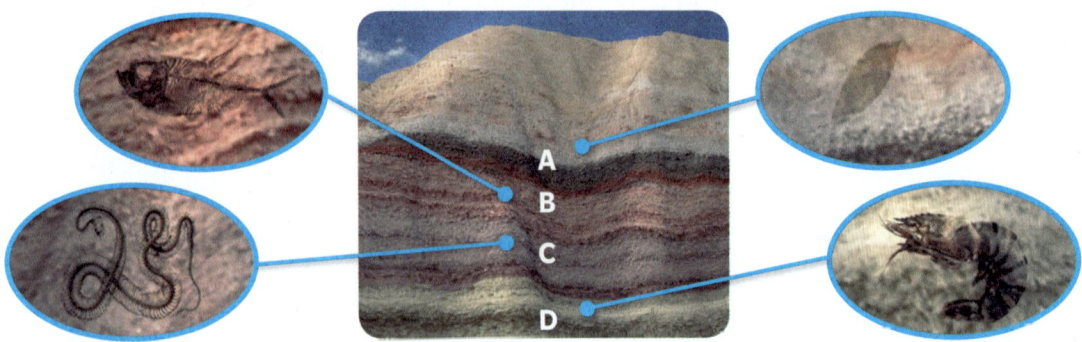

	Type of fossil	Where organism lived
Layer A	leaf	
Layer B	fish	
Layer C	snake	
Layer D	shrimp	

Fossils help scientists infer the characteristics of environments in which organisms lived. Scientists look for similar evidence of environmental characteristics when they study rock layers.

Identify Which rock layer is the oldest?

    a. Layer A   c. Layer C
    b. Layer B   d. Layer D

Analyze How do you know the layer you chose is the oldest?

    a. The oldest layer is usually on top.
    b. The oldest layer usually has land animals.
    c. The oldest layer is usually on the bottom.
    d. The oldest layer is between layers of limestone.

Infer Use the evidence to identify the oldest type of environment represented in these rock layers.

    a. desert   c. forest
    b. saltwater sea   d. mountain

Evaluate Look at the four environments below, and read their descriptions. Use the rock layers on the previous page as evidence to number the environments in order of age, with 1 being the oldest.

This area was once covered by a freshwater lake. Many fish, turtles, and other aquatic animals lived here at that time. Terrestrial animals also lived on the land around the lake. They used the lake as a drinking source.

Willow trees once grew here. At the time, the climate was much warmer than it is today. It had a temperate to subtropical environment, unlike today. Summers were hot and humid, and winters were mild but sometimes cool. Some trees lost their leaves in the winter.

The area was once covered by a saltwater sea. Many saltwater animals lived in the water, including clams, shrimp, sharks, and other fish.

At another time, the area was covered by a cypress forest. The ground was moist. Once in a while, organisms became trapped in the mud in this environment.

LESSON 3 • Rock Layers Record Landform Changes

Layering Up

When you dig deep enough into rock layers, you can discover patterns. These patterns can reveal a lot about the kinds of changes that took place on Earth's surface over long periods. Recall that processes such as weathering, erosion, and deposition can add and remove rock layers. Think about how scientists can use fossils as evidence to identify places where these kinds of changes have occurred.

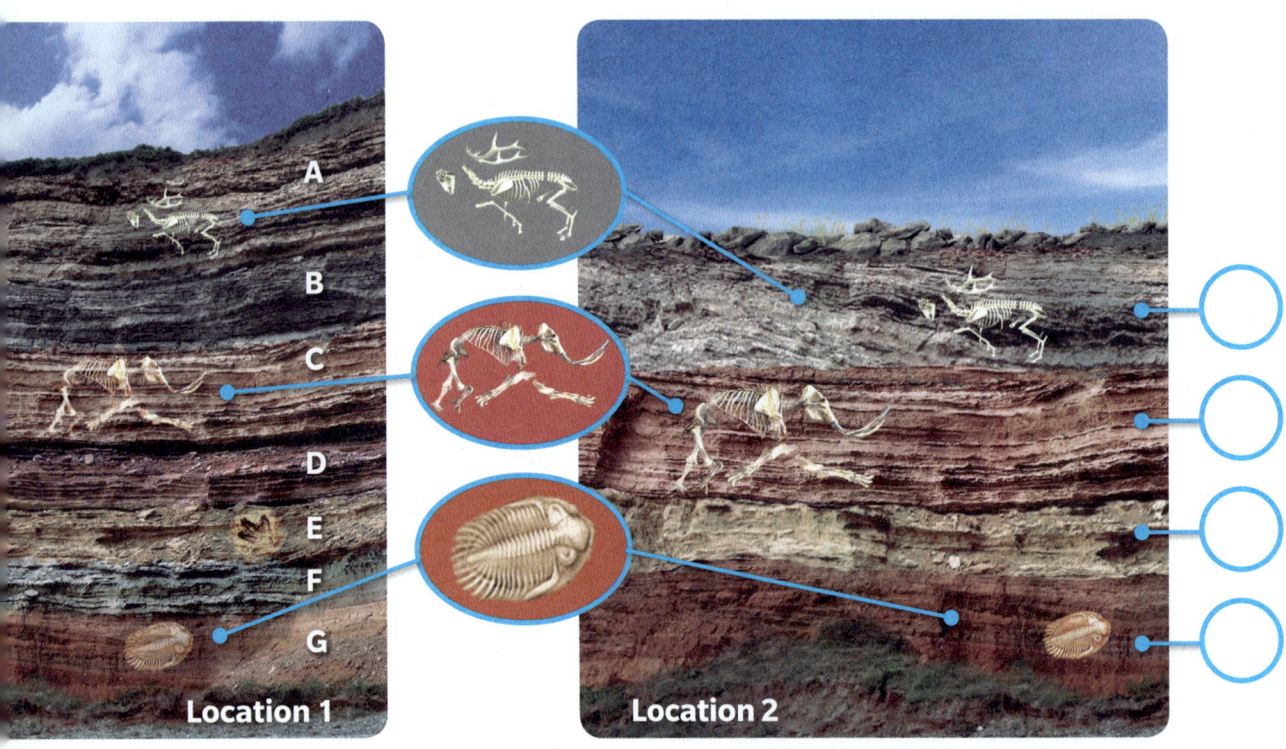

Location 1

Location 2

Identify Study the rock formations at locations 1 and 2. Use the fossils and your understanding of how layers form to write the correct letters in the circles to identify the rock layers present at both locations.

Write a claim about why you placed each letter where you did. Support your claim with evidence and reasoning.

_____

_____

_____

_____

LESSON 3 • Rock Layers Record Landform Changes

Rock Layers

Breaks, gaps, and other patterns in rock layers can indicate past weathering and erosion. Look at the images below. Think about how erosion has revealed the history of the western United States, resulting in landforms such as the Grand Canyon, in Arizona.

Over a long time, water cut deep through the Colorado plateau to form the Grand Canyon.

Today, dozens of rock layers are visible in the Grand Canyon.

Rock Formations and Forces

Rock formations are like books that contain chapters about Earth's history. They can record changes caused by natural forces strong enough to bend and break rock.

Earthquakes are caused by forces in Earth's interior. These forces can change the position of rock. Evidence of this motion is recorded in the rock layers.

LESSON 3 • Rock Layers Record Landform Changes

Rocked and Rolled

The same forces that cause earthquakes also cause rock layers to bend, break, fold, and tilt, which form various features. Factors such as rock's composition and its depth below Earth's surface affect which features form.

Deep below Earth's surface, under high heat and pressure, forces can cause rocks to bend and fold.

Near the surface, forces cause faults, or cracks, along which large blocks of rock can move.

Making Sense

You've explored how fossils within rock layers can be used as evidence of change. How do your findings help you understand how the footprints were made on the vertical rock wall?

 How do people record events that happened to them in the past? Why is it important to keep records of things that happened long ago? Share your ideas with a classmate.

Name _____

Lesson Check

Can You Explain It?

How do you think these prints can help scientists understand more about changes to Earth's surface?

Be sure to do the following:

- Discuss what is unusual about the orientation of the rock layers.
- Describe how this is evidence of changes in the environment.

Now I know or think that _____

_____

_____

_____

_____

Making Connections

Fossils can be used as evidence to identify if an environment has changed. This whale fossil was found in the dessert. How is this similar to footprints on the rock wall?

_____

_____

_____

_____

LESSON 3 • Rock Layers Record Landform Changes

Checkpoints

1. Scientists examine the patterns of fossils of organisms that lived at the same time period around the world and where they are found. How could scientists use these patterns to explain where they are found?

    a. They are found in similar rock layers.
    b. They are the same shapes and sizes.
    c. They are all copies of real fossils.
    d. They are found at similar times.

2. Why are the patterns in fossil evidence important to understanding Earth's past?

    _____
    _____
    _____
    _____
    _____
    _____

3. Identify which of these are patterns within rock layers.
    Circle all that apply.

    a. They are always flat.
    b. They can be different ages.
    c. They can change only during earthquakes.
    d. They can change slowly or quickly.
    e. They can bend or break.
    f. They all contain the same type of rock.

LESSON 3 • Rock Layers Record Landform Changes

4. Observe the patterns in the rock layers. Which fossil do you think is the oldest? Use evidence to support your claim.

_____

_____

_____

_____

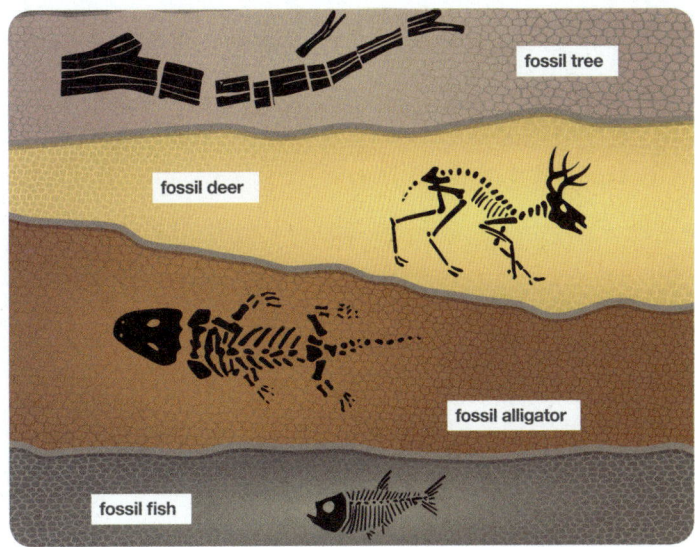

5. Which of the following could be used as evidence to explain why using fossils to learn about past environments may have limitations? Choose all that apply.

   a. Fossils are not common in many places.
   b. Fossils might indicate more than one type of environment.
   c. Fossils do not show enough detail to identify an environment.
   d. There are many different types of fossils.
   e. Fossils are often missing pieces or parts.

6. Construct an explanation of how rock layers form using the patterns in the layers as evidence of sudden change, such as an earthquake.

_____

_____

_____

_____

_____

LESSON 3 • Rock Layers Record Landform Changes

Name _____

Unit Review

1. Describe how you can investigate the effects of weathering on rock.

   _____

   _____

2. Forces on Earth's surface can cause it to change. Identify two different forces, and tell how they cause changes to Earth's surface.

   _____

   _____

3. Which forces cause changes to large landforms on Earth's surface that happen quickly? Choose all that apply.

   a. earthquakes   c. wind

   b. landslides   d. glaciers

4. Study the photo at the right. What is causing the change in the sidewalk? Support your claim with evidence.

   _____

   _____

   _____

5. Wind can cause changes to Earth's surface at different rates. What is the relationship between wind speed and how quickly Earth's surface changes?

   _____

   _____

   _____

6. What phenomenon caused this landscape to change?

   a. deposition
   b. glacial erosion
   c. topography
   d. flooding

7. You have investigated environments in which organisms lived millions of years ago. How can you tell the environment shown in the picture has changed over time? Support your claim with evidence.

8. Describe a model that you might use to represent the relationship between weathering, erosion, and deposition.

_____

_____

_____

_____

9. Suppose you are studying a rock formation composed of multiple layers. Some layers are thicker than others, and they have different colors and particle sizes. Make a claim supported by evidence about the processes that created this rock formation.

_____

_____

_____

_____

10. Which of the following played a role in the formation of the landscape shown on the right? Circle all that apply.

    a. erosion

    b. eruption

    c. fossil

    d. deposition

    e. weathering

In Unit 4, you used evidence of patterns in rocks to explain how Earth's landforms change through time. In this unit, you will analyze maps to describe patterns of Earth's land and water features. You will also design solutions to natural hazards that are caused by Earth processes.

UNIT 5 Earth's Features and Resources

Lesson 1
Patterns on Earth 222

Lesson 2
Reducing the Impacts of
Natural Hazards 238

Lesson 3
Resources 256

Unit Review 278

LESSON 1
Patterns on Earth

What do you notice about this map?

I notice _____

_____

_____

_____

What do you wonder about what the map shows?

I wonder _____

_____

_____

_____

Can You Explain It?

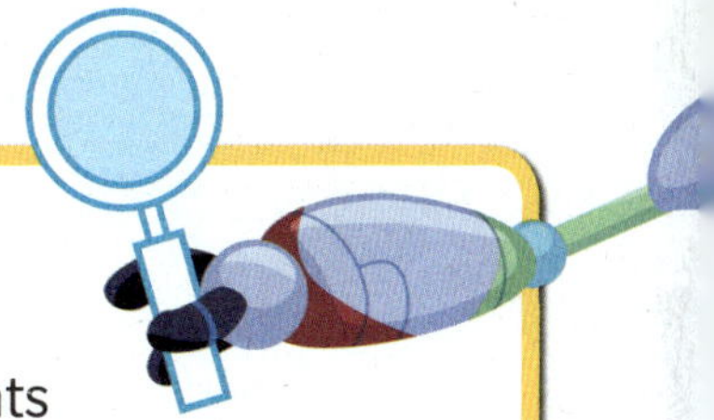

How do maps help people see patterns of land formations and events that appear on Earth but are not always visible?

Sketch, write, or model your answer.

HANDS-ON ACTIVITY

Tracking Quakes

While earthquakes happen all over the world, they usually happen in predictable places. Scientists detect about 50 earthquakes each day. Now you have the chance to look for patterns among recent earthquakes. Examine data to find out where most earthquakes occur.

Form a question Ask a question about where earthquakes occur.

_____
_____
_____
_____

Did you know?

The strongest recorded earthquake occurred in Chile in 1960, and seismographs recorded seismic waves that shook the entire planet for days.

224 LESSON 1 • Patterns on Earth

POSSIBLE MATERIALS
- [ ] world map with country boundaries
- [ ] data on earthquakes from the USGS

STEP 1 **Investigate your question** With a partner, find data on 20 earthquakes that have occurred during the past week.

STEP 2 **Record your data** Make a data table. For each of the 20 earthquakes, record the date, magnitude, and location. Use additional paper as needed.

LESSON 1 • Patterns on Earth

STEP 3 **Analyze your data** Plot the earthquake locations on your world map. You should use one symbol for each location of an earthquake. In which part of the world did most of the earthquakes occur? Do you see a pattern in the location of the earthquakes?

_____

_____

_____

Of the earthquakes you plotted, in what type of area did most occur?

_____

_____

_____

What does an earthquake's magnitude indicate? Research the term, if needed.

_____

_____

Make a **claim** about earthquakes. What **evidence** do you have that most earthquakes occur in certain parts of the world? Explain your **reasoning**.

_____

_____

_____

_____

 In the space below, list two examples of good communication and teamwork that you followed during this investigation.

_____

_____

_____

_____

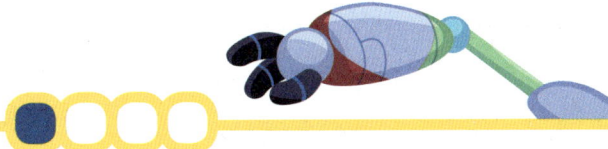

Making Sense

How does your claim or the evidence you gathered in this investigation help you begin to explain how maps help people see patterns on Earth?

_____

_____

_____

_____

LESSON 1 • Patterns on Earth

HANDS-ON ACTIVITY

Volcanic Eruptions

An erupting volcano is an amazing sight, especially at night. Volcanoes form when pressure below Earth's surface causes hot, molten rock called *lava* to flow onto the land. They also form when ash explodes onto Earth's surface. Volcanoes are found only in certain places on Earth.

Form a question What question do you have about where volcanoes are found?

_____
_____
_____
_____

Did you know?

Earth has some large volcanoes, but the biggest volcano in our solar system is Olympus Mons on the planet Mars.

POSSIBLE MATERIALS
- ☐ world map with country boundaries
- ☐ data on volcanoes from the Smithsonian

Investigate your question With a partner, find data on 10 volcanoes that have erupted in the last week, or are still erupting. Record your data in a data table. Then, plot the eruption locations on the same map you plotted your earthquake locations on. Do you see a pattern in the location of the volcanic eruptions?

___

___

In what type of area did most of the plotted volcanoes occur? Support your **claim** with **evidence,** and explain your **reasoning**.

___

___

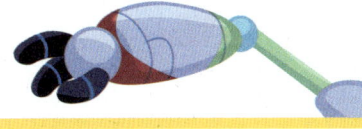

Making Sense

How does your claim or the evidence you gathered in this investigation help you begin to explain how maps help people see patterns on Earth?

___

___

___

LESSON 1 • Patterns on Earth

EXPLORATION

By Land or By Sea

Shaking and Melting

Earthquakes and volcanoes occur all around the world, but they do not occur everywhere. You see patterns when earthquakes and volcanoes happen in the same kinds of locations again and again.

Up and Down

Besides earthquakes and volcanoes, features found on Earth's surface include mountains and trenches.

Earthquakes occur when large blocks of rock shift and release stored energy. They cause the ground to shake.

When volcanoes erupt, lava flows onto Earth's surface. Ash from volcanic eruptions can travel great distances.

 Mountains can form on land or underwater. Some are very tall and jagged, while others are smaller and rounded.

 An **ocean trench** is a long, deep, narrow valley found on the ocean floor. The Mariana Trench in the Pacific Ocean is the deepest ocean trench.

Mapping the Ocean Floor

The ocean floor has many interesting features—mountains, trenches, and volcanoes, just to name a few. But how do we know this?

Multibeam sonar is a technology that uses sound waves to determine how deep the ocean floor is. A multibeam sonar signal extends out from a ship in a fanlike pattern. The signal returns data about the features on the ocean floor. Scientists use this information to make ocean floor maps.

Evaluate What is an advantage of using sonar to map the ocean floor? What is a disadvantage?

___

___

 Discuss your answer with your group. Provide constructive feedback for each answer, and make sure everyone has a chance to speak.

Making Sense

You've explored land formations and events that occur under water and on land. How do your findings help you begin to explain how maps help people see patterns on Earth?

___

___

___

___

___

LESSON 1 • Patterns on Earth

EXPLORATION

Finding Patterns

Patterns on the Ocean Floor

This map shows earthquakes and other features on the ocean floor.

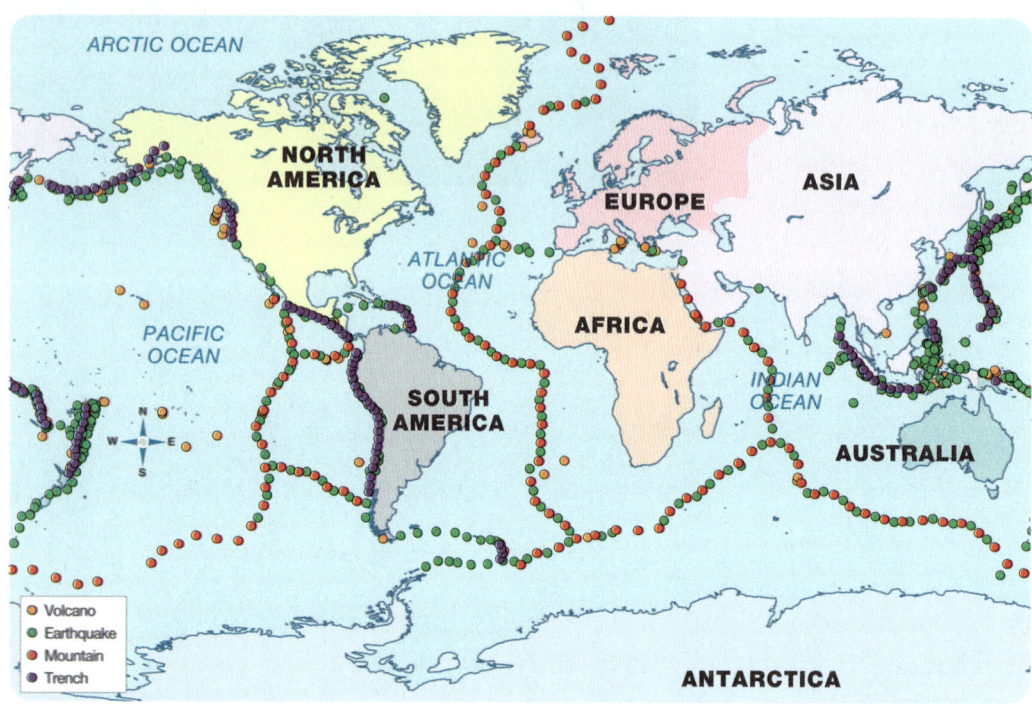

Most underwater volcanoes occur near islands, and a few occur in the middle of the ocean. Many underwater mountain ranges are found near the centers of the ocean. Ocean trenches are common near coastlines.

Analyze Compare the locations of earthquakes and volcanoes in the map above with the locations on land on the next page. Do earthquakes and volcanoes follow the same pattern on land as they do in the ocean?

Argue Compare the map above with the maps on the next page. Do the mountain ranges on land follow the same pattern as mountain ranges in the ocean?

Patterns on Land

You've discovered that mountains, earthquakes, and volcanoes can occur in the ocean. They also occur on land. Where on Earth are they more likely to occur?

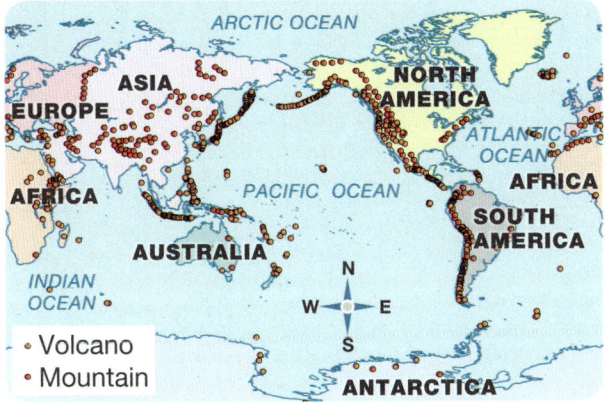

This map shows the locations of volcanoes and mountains that have formed on land.

This map shows earthquake epicenters, or where earthquakes have started, on land.

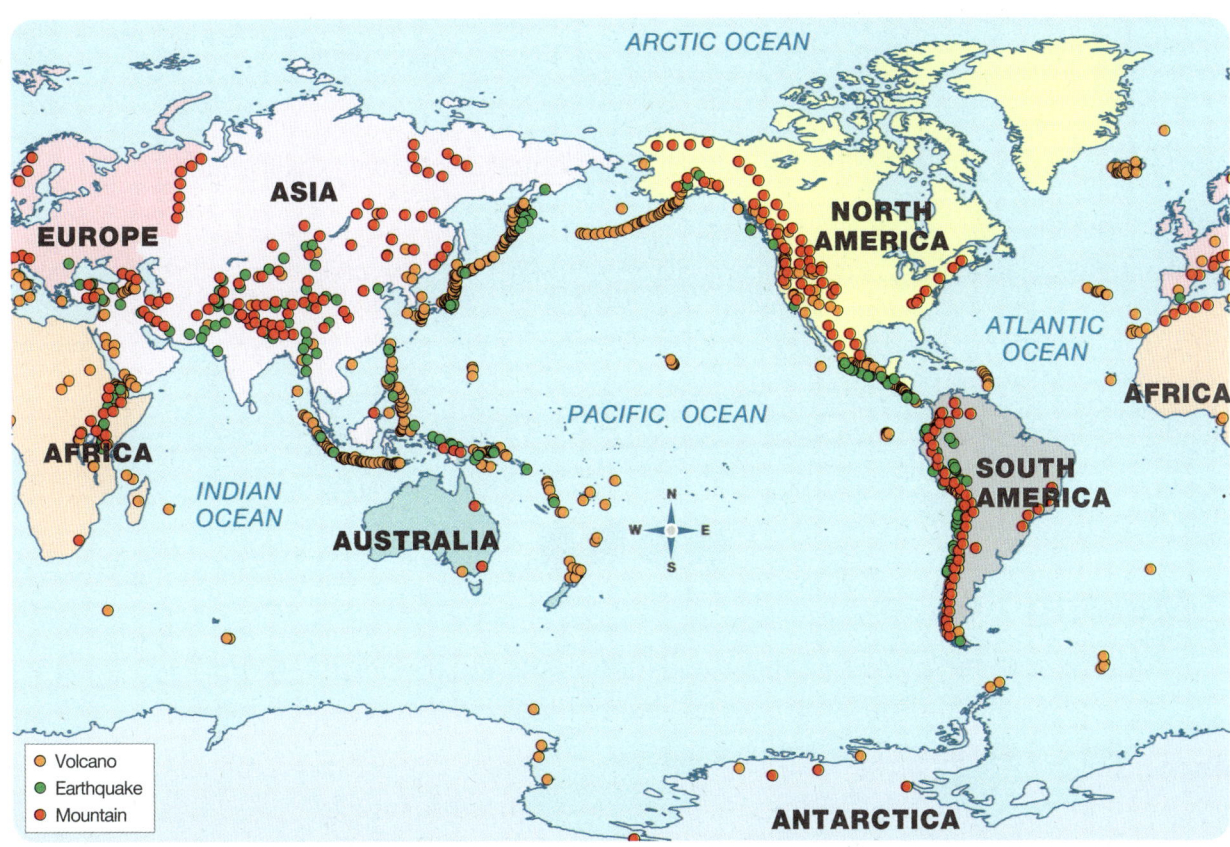

Earthquakes on land are most likely to occur near the edges of continents. Volcanoes on land often are located near the edges of continents and the area around the Pacific Ocean has many. This area is known as the *Ring of Fire*. Mountains on land are found in the center and near the edges of continents.

LESSON 1 • Patterns on Earth

California Quake Plot

An earthquake epicenter is the place on Earth's surface right above where an earthquake starts. People mapped Earth with lines of longitude that go around Earth vertically and lines of latitude that run horizontally. Every location on Earth can be identified by the intersection of the line of latitude and longitude.

Apply Plot the epicenters of these earthquakes on the map.

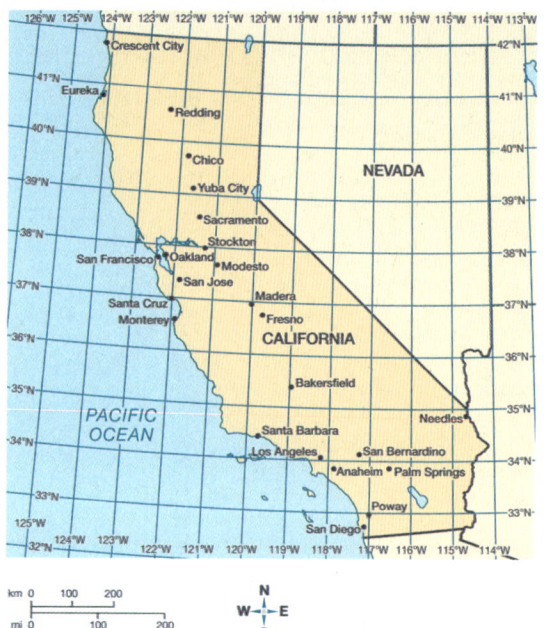

Earthquake Epicenters		
Latitude (°N)	Longtitude (°W)	Year
36.20	120.80	1857
32.55	115.65	1892
37.70	122.50	1906
41.12	124.67	1980
42.02	125.72	1991

Infer Use your map to describe the pattern of earthquake activity in California.

_____
_____
_____

Making Sense

You've explored maps that show land formations and events that occur underwater and on land. How do your findings help you begin to explain how maps help people see patterns on Earth?

_____
_____
_____

Name _____

Lesson Check

Can You Explain It?

Review your ideas from the beginning of this lesson about how maps help people see patterns on Earth. How have your ideas changed?

Be sure to do the following:
- Explain what this map shows.
- Interpret the map to describe patterns you otherwise would not be able to see.

Now I know or think that _____

_____

_____

Making Connections

This image shows the San Andreas Fault in California. Explain how a map could be used to identify patterns that form along the fault, patterns that you otherwise would not be able to see.

_____

_____

_____

_____

LESSON 1 • Patterns on Earth   235

Checkpoints

1. Think of the patterns of Earth's features you identified in this lesson. Circle all the features that occur in the ocean.

   a. mountains

   b. ocean trenches

   c. volcanoes

   d. earthquakes

2. Circle the correct answer. Most volcanoes and earthquakes occur in patterns around the

   a. middle of the Atlantic Ocean

   b. edges of the Pacific Ocean

   c. coastlines of Africa

   d. center of South America

3. Study the map. Which statements describe the information it shows? Circle all that apply.

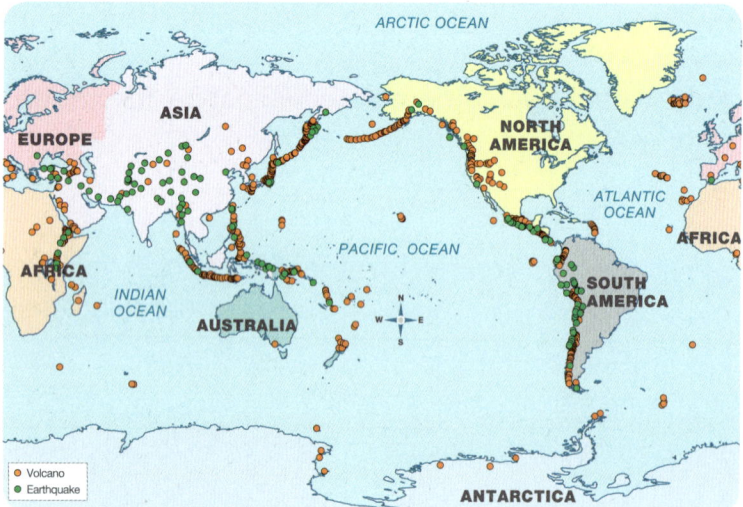

   a. It shows every volcano on Earth.

   b. It shows a pattern in the locations of volcanoes.

   c. It shows where every future earthquake will occur.

   d. It shows a pattern in the locations of past earthquakes.

4. Imagine you are piloting a submarine just above a somewhat flat area of the ocean floor. The ocean floor begins to slope downward. You cannot see the ocean floor anymore. It's as if you've glided off the peak of a steep mountain. A few minutes later, the submarine's sensors tell you the ocean floor is now 5 km deeper than your present depth. Based on these patterns, what landform is your submarine hovering over?

   a. a plain

   b. a mountain

   c. an ocean trench

   d. a volcano

5. Analyze the pattern you see on this map.

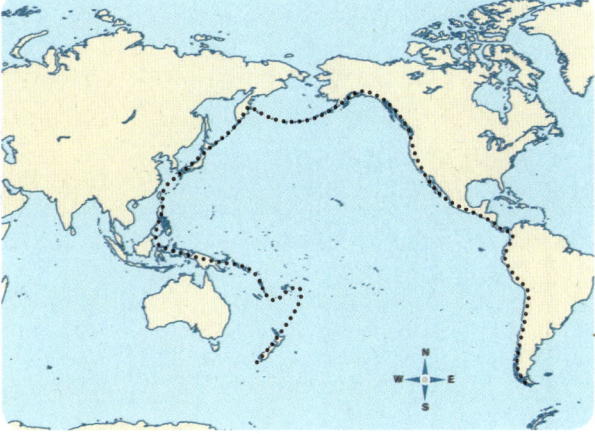

Why is the pattern shown on the map known as the Ring of Fire?

_____

_____

_____

6. Analyze the patterns you see on this map of ocean structures.

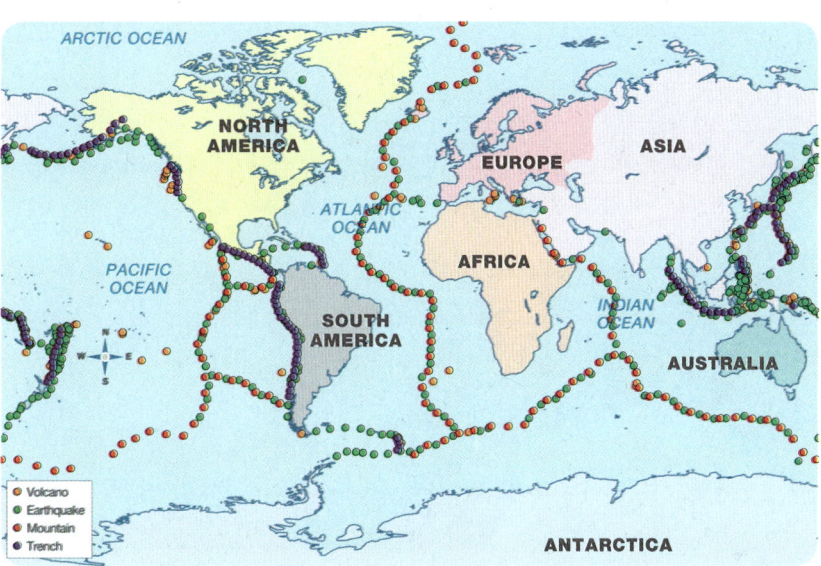

Identify the locations of volcanoes, earthquakes, mountains, and trenches.

_____

_____

_____

LESSON 2
Reducing the Impacts of Natural Hazards

What do you notice about what the men are doing?

I notice _____

_____

_____

_____

What do you wonder about what the men are doing?

I wonder _____

_____

_____

_____

Can You Explain It?

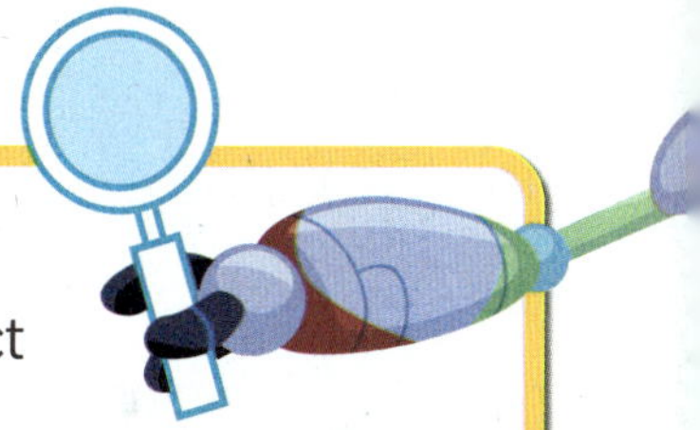

Putting metal over windows during a hurricane is one way to protect them from damage. How do scientists and engineers reduce the impacts of natural hazards?

Sketch, write, or model your answer.

LESSON 2 • Reducing the Impacts of Natural Hazards

HANDS-ON ACTIVITY

Engineer It
Strong, Stable Structures

At the University of California, San Diego, engineers construct buildings to test their ability to withstand earthquakes. After building the structures, they are put on a shake table that simulates an earthquake of different magnitudes, or strengths. Usually, the longer the building can withstand the shaking, the stronger it is.

Form a question Ask a question about the kinds of materials and structures that are better able to withstand earthquakes.

Did you know?

Wood and steel are often used in buildings in earthquake prone areas.

_____

_____

_____

POSSIBLE MATERIALS
- [ ] cardboard rolls
- [ ] building blocks or sticks
- [ ] paper
- [ ] chenille sticks
- [ ] yarn or string
- [ ] tape or glue

Explore

STEP 1 **Investigate your question**

In the space below, plan a fair test to gather evidence to help you determine the properties of buildings and building materials that are better able to withstand earthquakes. You may choose to write or draw the steps.

LESSON 2 • Reducing the Impacts of Natural Hazards

Make and Test

STEP 2 **Organize your data** Carry out your plan and record your results. Use this space to organize your data.

Make a **claim** about buildings and building materials that are better able to withstand earthquakes. Support your claim with **evidence** from your investigation and explain your **reasoning**.

_____

_____

_____

Making Sense

How does your claim or the evidence you gathered in this investigation help you begin to explain how people can reduce the impacts of natural hazards?

_____

_____

_____

242 LESSON 2 • Reducing the Impacts of Natural Hazards

HANDS-ON ACTIVITY

Make Your Own Seismograph

The image above shows a room of seismographs. A seismograph is a machine that scientists use to detect and measure seismic waves. Seismic waves are a kind of wave that is usually caused by movements in Earth's crust, such as earthquakes, but they also can be caused by volcanoes, landslides, and explosions. Seismograms are the graphs that seismographs make.

Form a question Ask a question about a seismograph recording data about seismic waves.

Did you know?

Most seismograms are rarely recorded on paper nowadays. They typically record seismic wave data digitally. This makes it easier to analyze using a computer.

LESSON 2 • Reducing the Impacts of Natural Hazards

POSSIBLE MATERIALS
- ☐ shoebox without lid
- ☐ construction paper
- ☐ yarn or string
- ☐ ruler
- ☐ clear adhesive tape
- ☐ fine line marker
- ☐ pointed tip scissors
- ☐ 2 rubber bands

Build the Seismograph

STEP 1 Use a ruler to measure a 10 cm cutting line along the center of the bottom edge of each long side of the box. Cut a slit along each cutting line.

STEP 2 Cut the paper into 9 cm wide strips. Attach the pieces together with tape to form one strip. Insert the strip of paper into the slits so that each end extends out of the slits.

STEP 3 Attach two rubber bands so that the bands are stretched wide to the sides of the two box slits.

STEP 4 Cut two pieces of yarn or string. Tie the marker into place between the rubber bands. The tip should lightly rest on the paper in the box.

STEP 5 **Investigate your question** Working together, one partner jiggles the box while the other pulls the strip through to get a seismogram reading on the paper.

Make sure to communicate with your partner and take turns when using the seismograph.

244 LESSON 2 • Reducing the Impacts of Natural Hazards

Describe what the seismogram looks like when you produce a "weak" earthquake. Describe what the seismogram looks like when you produce a "strong" earthquake.

_____
_____
_____
_____

Explain one way your seismograph could be improved.

_____
_____

Draw conclusions Make a **claim** about how seismographs record data about seismic waves. Support your claim with **evidence** from your investigation and explain your **reasoning**.

_____
_____
_____
_____

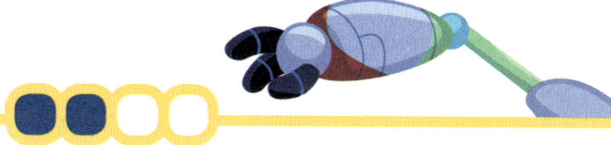

Making Sense

How do your findings help you explain how people can reduce the impacts of natural hazards?

_____
_____
_____

LESSON 2 • Reducing the Impacts of Natural Hazards 245

EXPLORATION

Natural Hazards

Nature's Dangers

Earth has many processes that affect its surface. Some of these processes can result in natural hazards. A **natural hazard** is an Earth process that threatens people and property.

 When a volcano erupts, it can release lava, rocks, ash, and poisonous gases. These can be dangerous to people and surrounding property.

 Landslides are falling or flowing soil, mud, rocks, or snow. Rock slides and snow avalanches occur on steep slopes, but mud can flow on a gentle slope.

 During an earthquake, the ground shakes violently. This shaking can destroy buildings and injure people.

 During a wildfire, an area of forest, shrub, or grassland burns out of control. Buildings can be destroyed, and people have to leave.

 A hurricane is a strong storm with dangerous winds and heavy rains. It is not safe to be outdoors during a hurricane.

 A tsunami is a powerful type of wave. It rushes onto the ocean shore like a high flood. It can have enough force to smash buildings.

 During a drought, there is much less water than usual. People and animals struggle to have enough water.

 During a flood, water covers the land and may get into homes as well. Floodwater can ruin property and threaten people's safety.

Cause and Effect

The cause of every natural hazard is related to an Earth process. The effects of these events can be very destructive.

Read about the natural hazards. Then match each hazard with its effect.

Volcanic eruptions occur when molten rock bursts through an opening in Earth's crust. The hot lava can cause wildfires. Falling ash can cause landslides.

Sometimes, enormous pieces of Earth's crust suddenly snap past each other, causing an earthquake. The ground shakes so hard that buildings can collapse.

Landslides can be triggered by volcanic eruption or earthquakes. They can knock down trees, and they can bury homes and other property.

Wildfires are caused by human activities, volcanic eruptions, dry conditions, and lightning. They can destroy environments and homes as well as cause landslides.

A hurricane forms as the energy in warm ocean water fuels strong winds and heavy rains. It causes storm surges, flooding, landslides, and wind damage.

Droughts are caused by periods of little or no rain. Droughts can last years. Dead, dry plants burn easily, so droughts can lead to wildfires.

LESSON 2 • Reducing the Impacts of Natural Hazards

Tsunamis are a series of giant waves, caused by undersea earthquakes, landslides, or volcanic eruptions. Tsunamis move onto shore, washing away almost anything in their paths.

River flooding is caused by heavy rain or snowmelt. Coastal flooding is caused by storm surges. Floodwater can damage structures and cause landslides.

Natural Hazard	Effect
volcanic eruption	rock and soil slides down steep slopes
wildfire	plants, animals, and people do not have enough water
earthquake	strong winds, storm surge, heavy rains
landslide	trees and homes burn up
hurricane	molten rock comes through an opening in Earth's crust and causes wildfires
drought	the ground shakes hard enough to destroy buildings

Making Sense

How do your findings help you explain how natural hazards can affect people?

_____
_____
_____

LESSON 2 • Reducing the Impacts of Natural Hazards

EXPLORATION

Natural Hazard Solutions

Expect the Unexpected

Think back to the metal on the window at the beginning of the lesson. To reduce the impact of a hurricane, metal is used because it is stronger than the window. You can't prevent natural hazards from happening. They are the results of Earth's processes. However, you can prepare for natural hazards and plan for how to be safe when they do occur.

Earthquake-Resistant Buildings

How would you design an earthquake-resistant building? When engineers design buildings to be resistant to earthquakes, they consider many factors. Look at the picture to learn more.

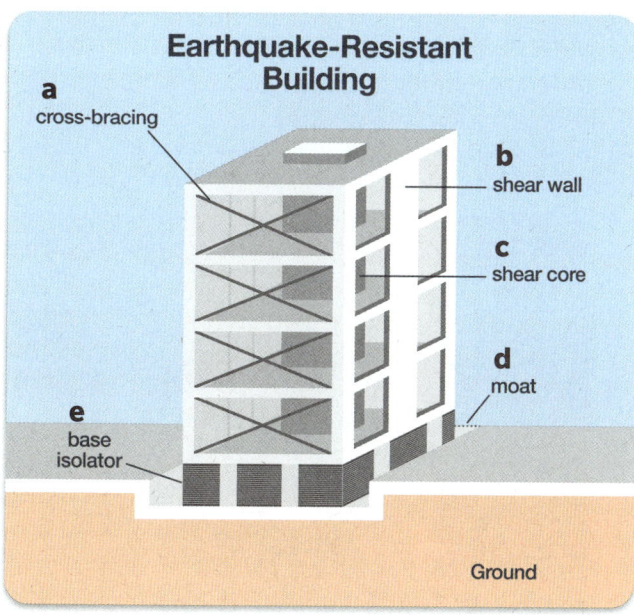

a. Cross-braces are diagonal. They help reinforce the building and increase its stability.

b. Shear walls are vertical walls. They help make the building solid and stiff. They increase the ability of the structure to withstand rocking.

c. In the middle of a building, you might find a shear core. This is an inside structure made out of shear walls. You might find a shear core around an elevator.

d. A moat is an area around the outside of a building. A moat protects the building from damage by nearby buildings that are not earthquake resistant.

e. A base isolator separates the building from the ground. A base isolator is made to absorb the movement of the earthquake.

 Natural hazards can be scary for kids and grown ups, too! Turn to a partner and talk about what you can do about natural hazards to feel less scared when they occur.

LESSON 2 • Reducing the Impacts of Natural Hazards

What's the Pattern?

Because we can't prevent natural hazards, scientists study patterns that serve as warning signs. It's important to predict these hazards so that people can be prepared or get to safety during a natural hazard event.

Scientists can predict a volcanic eruption if they see a pattern of movement of the ground, earthquakes, and release of volcanic gases. All of these can be detected by scientific tools.

Warning signs for earthquakes include past earthquakes in the area and strain in Earth's crust. Movement in Earth's crust is measured using modern technology.

Landslides happen suddenly, with little warning. They often occur with earthquakes, volcanoes, heavy rains, and wildfires.

Wildfires occur when there is very little rainfall but heavy winds. Under dry conditions, once a wildfire has started satellites or aircraft can find it. Then people are alerted and take action.

Tsunamis typically form when earthquakes move large volumes of water. Rising or falling water levels can indicate a tsunami is coming. A warning system tells countries when coasts are in danger.

Warning signs for floods include heavy rainfall, levee or dam failure, and early snowmelt. Warnings are based on past flooding patterns and readings from scientific equipment.

Scientists detect and track hurricanes using satellites and radar. Warning signs can include an increase in ocean swell, wave frequency, wind speed, and rainfall.

Weather and climate patterns, including rainfall and temperature, can help determine areas at risk for drought. Reservoirs can save water for periods when there are droughts.

Disaster Supply Kit

Select one type of natural hazard. Brainstorm and research what supplies would be important to include in a disaster supply kit for this type of hazard. Draw a diagram of your supply kit. Identify the type of hazard it is designed for. List the things you will include, and write an explanation of why each item is important.

LESSON 2 • Reducing the Impacts of Natural Hazards

Reducing Impacts with Technology

Humans cannot prevent earthquakes, volcanic eruptions, or other natural hazards. But technology can help us be safer from natural hazards. As you read the captions, underline the name of the technology and circle the name of the natural hazard it keeps us safer from.

When molten rock moves upward, it tilts the ground around it. A tiltmeter records these changes, helping scientists predict eruptions.

Seismograph readings show the size and location of an earthquake's source, including how deep underground it is.

If a tsunami passes under a deep-ocean detection buoy, the buoy sends data to a warning center. The buoys help scientists predict when tsunamis might reach shore.

Piles and retaining walls are built to keep unstable rocks and soil from sliding down a hillside during a landslide.

Making Sense

How do your findings help you explain how people use technology to reduce the impacts of natural hazards?

_____

_____

Name _____

Lesson Check

Can You Explain It?

What are some ways people can reduce the impacts of natural hazards? Be sure to do the following:

- Describe several natural hazards.
- Describe ways that the impact of natural hazards can be lessened.
- Explain how engineering processes can reduce the impact of natural hazards.

Now I know or think that _____

_____

_____

_____

_____

_____

_____

Making Connections

People developed various solutions to reduce the impacts of natural hazards. How is this house similar to the man installing the shutters at the beginning of the lesson? How is it different?

_____

_____

_____

LESSON 2 • Reducing the Impacts of Natural Hazards

Checkpoints

1. Match each word with the correct picture of a technology that can reduce the impact of that type of hazard.

Natural Hazards

volcanic eruption

tsunami

earthquake

landslide

2. Use the word bank to write the most likely cause of each of these effects.

   | earthquake   volcano   both |

   a. landslide
   b. crumpled roads
   c. building collapse
   d. release of poisonous gases

3. Circle all of the natural hazards that are most likely to be the direct cause of a wildfire.
   a. earthquake
   b. volcano
   c. landslide
   d. lightning strike

4. Circle the natural hazards that can occur when there is very little or no rain.
   a. drought
   b. earthquake
   c. volcano
   d. wildfire

5. Identify the hazard for which each technology is a solution. Then explain the effect of the technology before or during a hazard event.

Hazard	Technology	How it is used
	deep-ocean buoys	
	tiltmeter	
	seismograph	

6. Use examples to explain why understanding the causes and effects of natural hazards is important to helping people stay safe.

_____
_____
_____

7. Individual landslides cannot be predicted, but scientists know the occurrence of certain hazards can make a landslide more likely. Identify one of those hazards, and explain how it can trigger a landslide.

_____
_____
_____

8. The Richter scale is used to measure and compare earthquakes. Each magnitude on the Richter scale is 10 times as great as the one before it. So a magnitude 3 earthquake is 10 times as strong as a magnitude 2 earthquake. A magnitude 3 earthquake is also 100 times as strong as a magnitude 1 earthquake.

Use the table to determine the magnitude of an earthquake in which you felt the ground shake.

Magnitude	Ground Shaking
1–3	not felt
3–4	weak
4–5	light/moderate
5–6	strong/very strong
6–7	very strong/severe
7+	severe/violent/extreme

_____
_____

LESSON 2 • Reducing the Impacts of Natural Hazards

LESSON 3

Resources

What do these cars run on?

What do you notice about the two cars?

I notice _____
_____
_____
_____

What do you wonder about the two cars?

I wonder _____
_____
_____
_____

Can You Explain It?

How do new technologies allow for new sources of fuel?

Sketch, write, or model your answer.

HANDS-ON ACTIVITY

Modeling Energy Resource Use

Coal is a nonrenewable resource people use for heat and electricity. A **nonrenewable resource** is a resource that, once used, cannot be replaced in a reasonable amount of time. Digging for coal is called mining. To obtain coal, people dig deep into the earth or strip away the earth's surface. While nonrenewable resources are easy to obtain at first, their availability changes over time.

Form a question Ask a question about how nonrenewable resource availability changes over time with human use.

_____
_____
_____

Did you know?

It can take thousands to millions of years for nonrenewable resources to form!

258 LESSON 3 • Resources

POSSIBLE MATERIALS
- [ ] small paper cups
- [ ] counting chips
- [ ] posterboard
- [ ] drawing and writing tools
- [ ] other items you need to complete your plan

STEP 1 **Investigate your question** Your teacher will give you counting chips to represent your coal supply. In the space below, plan how you will use a model to investigate your question. List any additional materials you will use. You may choose to write or draw the steps.

STEP 2 **Organize your data** Use this space to organize your data.

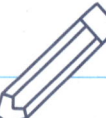

STEP 3 **Analyze your data** Describe what your model shows about how nonrenewable resource use affects availability over time.

_____

_____

_____

STEP 4 **Draw conclusions** Share your data with other groups. Explain any differences or similarities among the groups' data.

_____

_____

_____

Make a **claim** about nonrenewable resource supplies and their use. Support your claim with **evidence** from your investigation and explain your **reasoning**.

_____
_____
_____
_____
_____
_____

In the space below, give an example of how you may have handled any disagreements you had with your partner.

_____
_____

Making Sense

How does your claim or the evidence you gathered in this investigation help you begin to explain how new technologies allow for new energy sources?

_____
_____
_____
_____

HANDS-ON ACTIVITY

Engineer It
Running on Sunshine

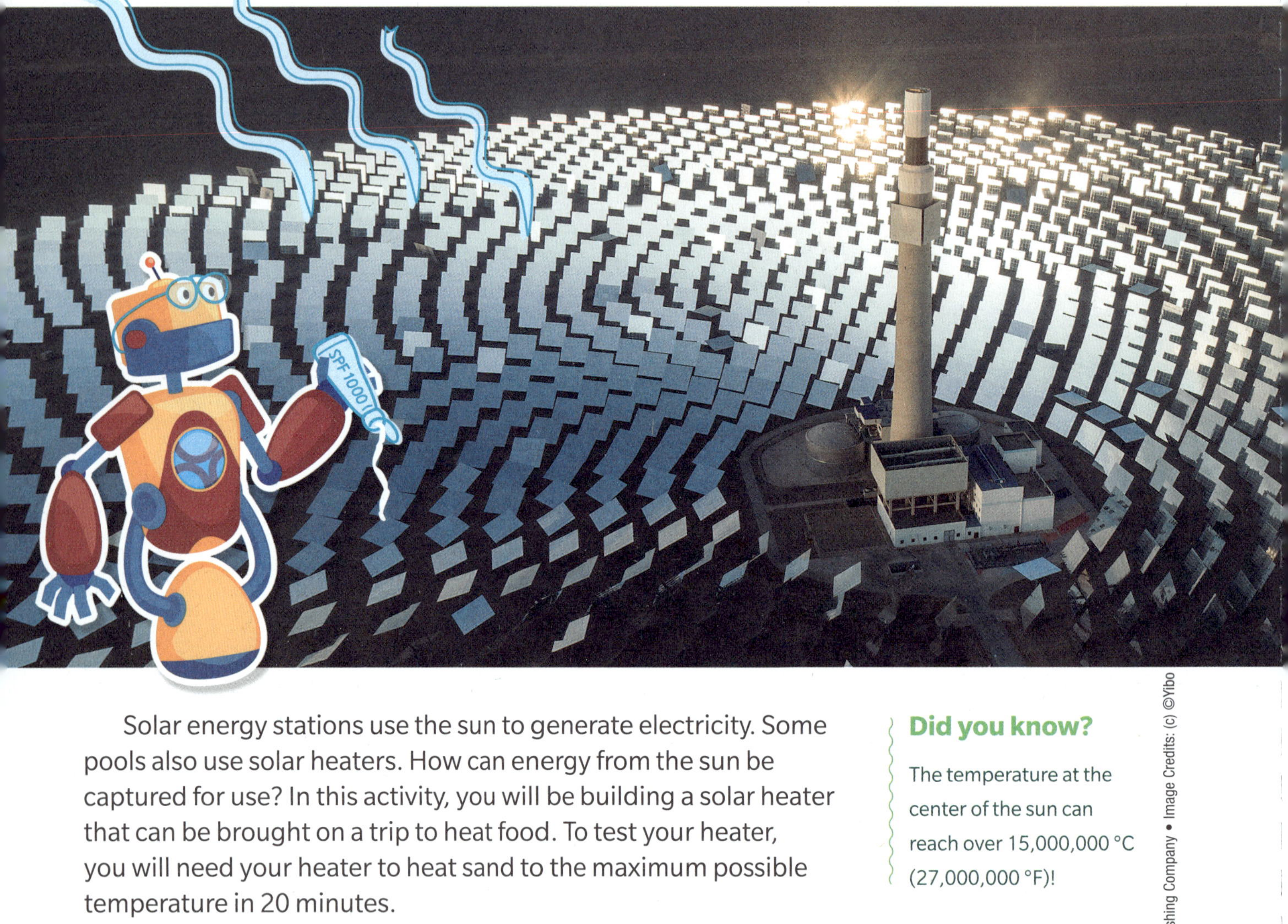

Solar energy stations use the sun to generate electricity. Some pools also use solar heaters. How can energy from the sun be captured for use? In this activity, you will be building a solar heater that can be brought on a trip to heat food. To test your heater, you will need your heater to heat sand to the maximum possible temperature in 20 minutes.

Form a question Ask a question about how you might use energy from the sun.

_____
_____
_____
_____

> **Did you know?**
>
> The temperature at the center of the sun can reach over 15,000,000 °C (27,000,000 °F)!

POSSIBLE MATERIALS

- ☐ sand container
- ☐ sand
- ☐ scissors
- ☐ tape
- ☐ thermometers
- ☐ timer or watch
- ☐ measuring cup
- ☐ two separate cups
- ☐ cardboard box
- ☐ black paint
- ☐ black construction paper
- ☐ plastic wrap
- ☐ packing peanuts
- ☐ newspaper
- ☐ cotton balls
- ☐ aluminum foil
- ☐ wax paper
- ☐ paper plates
- ☐ plastic shopping bags
- ☐ paper towels

Explore

STEP 1 — **Research** With your group, find more information about materials you can use to help you capture solar energy. Think about the color and texture of the materials you need.

STEP 2 — **Define the problem** What are your criteria for the solution? What are your constraints?

_____

_____

STEP 3 — **Brainstorm solutions** Talk about solutions for your device. Then, evaluate your solutions and choose the best one.

Make and Test

STEP 4 — **Develop and test a model** On a separate sheet of paper, draw your device with your group. Label its parts. Explain how you will test it. Get your teacher's approval before you follow your plan.

LESSON 3 • Resources   263

Build and test your device. Draw a data table where you will record your results.

Test your solar heater outside. Fill two separate cups with equal amounts of sand. Use the thermometers to record the starting temperature of the sand. Record the temperatures in the table under 0. Place the heater in bright sunlight. Place one cup of sand in the heater. Place the other in the sun nearby. Record the temperature of the sand in both cups every 5 minutes for 20 minutes.

How will you know whether your results are correct? What steps can you take to ensure your measurements are correct?

_____
_____
_____

What was the highest temperature you recorded? What was the difference between that temperature and your starting temperature?

_____
_____
_____

STEP 5

Evaluate Use the data from your test. Compare the sand inside the heater and the sand outside the heater. Did your materials help your heater work? If not, how could you improve your design?

_____
_____
_____
_____

Improve and Test

STEP 6 **Develop and test a new model** Develop a new model. Take the improved heater outside and retest. Record the temperature in the table every 5 minutes for 20 minutes. What improvement did you make to your design?

How well did your improved design meet the criteria and constraints? Explain.

_____

_____

STEP 7 **Draw conclusions** Compare your results to those of the other groups in your class. Did their solar heaters work better than yours? Why or why not?

_____

_____

Make a **claim** based on your investigation. Cite **evidence** from your design and other designs to support your claim. Explain your **reasoning**.

_____

_____

_____

Making Sense

How does your claim or the evidence you gathered in this investigation help you begin to explain how new technologies allow for new energy sources?

_____

_____

LESSON 3 • Resources

EXPLORATION

Materials We Use

Resources Around You

A **resource** is anything you use to live. Your house is a resource because it gives you shelter. Clothes are a resource because they keep you warm. A **natural resource** is a material from nature that people can use. Water, air, trees, wind, fossil fuels, minerals, and sunlight are all natural resources.

Crude oil formed mainly from the remains of tiny living things that lived in the sea and were buried under mud. It is used for heat and to fuel vehicles; it is also an ingredient in many products, such as plastics and paints.

Uranium is a natural element. It is not the remains of living things, but it is found in rocks formed billions of years ago. Uranium is used to produce nuclear energy that is used to generate electricity.

Coal formed from the buried remains of plants that died millions of years ago. In some places, coal is used for heating and for cooking.

Natural gas also formed from the remains of tiny living things. It is used for heat and as a fuel source for buses and other vehicles.

A **nonrenewable resource** is a resource that, once used, cannot be replaced in a reasonable amount of time. Fossil fuels, such as crude oil, coal, and natural gas, are nonrenewable resources. These fossil fuels are burned to release energy and generate electricity. They are considered nonrenewable because they take thousands to millions of years to form.

Where Are They Found?

Scientists and engineers use special nonrenewable resource technology to locate, remove, and process coal, crude oil, natural gas, and uranium from Earth. Each of these methods has certain benefits and risks. Some cause **pollution**, or waste products that damage ecosystems. According to the map, what resource is the rarest? Circle the resource on the map.

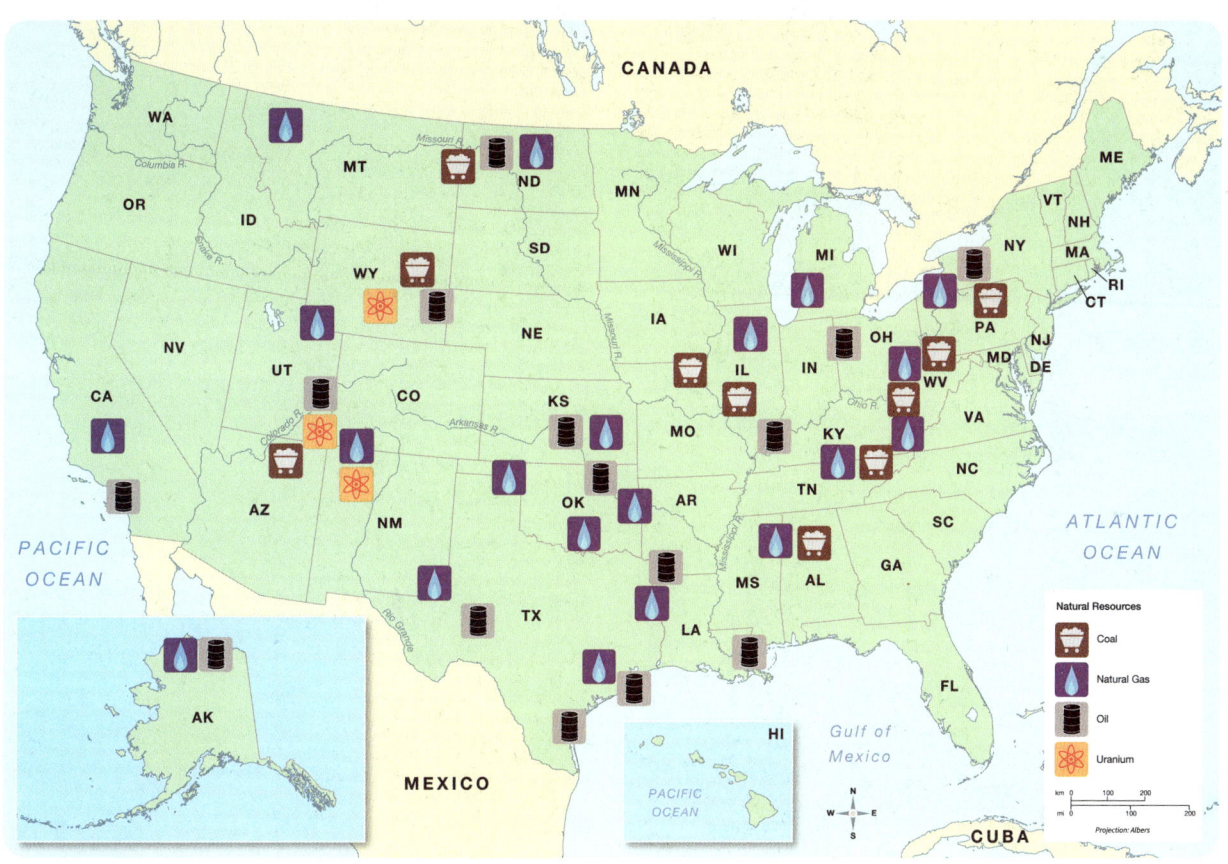

In the United States, crude oil is found mostly in the Midwest, South, Southwest, Alaska, and around Pennsylvania.

The Midwest, Montana, Wyoming, and Pennsylvania are the main sources of coal in the United States.

Natural gas is found mostly in Alaska, Texas, Oklahoma, New Mexico, Wyoming, and Louisiana. Some can also be found in the Midwest.

The United States was once the leader in uranium mining. Today, however, uranium is mined in only a few places, including New Mexico, Utah, and Wyoming.

Nonrenewable resources cannot replenish themselves. Efforts have been made to conserve fossil fuels to make sure people have enough energy for future needs. Conserving fossil fuels can also help limit the harmful effects of carbon dioxide and other gases, which are emitted when fossil fuels are burned.

LESSON 3 • Resources

Collecting and Processing

Nonrenewable resources are first removed from Earth's crust. Then they can be used by electricity-generating stations to provide electricity to homes and businesses. Explore the systems below to discover more about how these resources are collected and processed.

Gasoline used as fuel in vehicles comes from crude oil. Crude oil is pumped from underground wells, including wells that are underwater. This oil is also burned to generate electricity.

Uranium is mined from rocks and is used to produce large amounts of energy. The energy is then provided to homes and businesses for heat and electricity.

Coal is mined from deposits in layers of rocks. It is taken to electricity-generating stations to be burned and converted to electrical energy.

Natural gas is extracted from rocks deep underground. It is then transported by pipeline and burned to generate electricity.

Making Sense

How does your understanding of nonrenewable resources help you explain how new technologies allow for new sources of fuel?

EXPLORATION

Exploring Renewable Resources

Use It Again

Explore below to find out more about renewable energy sources. Then write the letter that describes each source next to the picture that shows it.

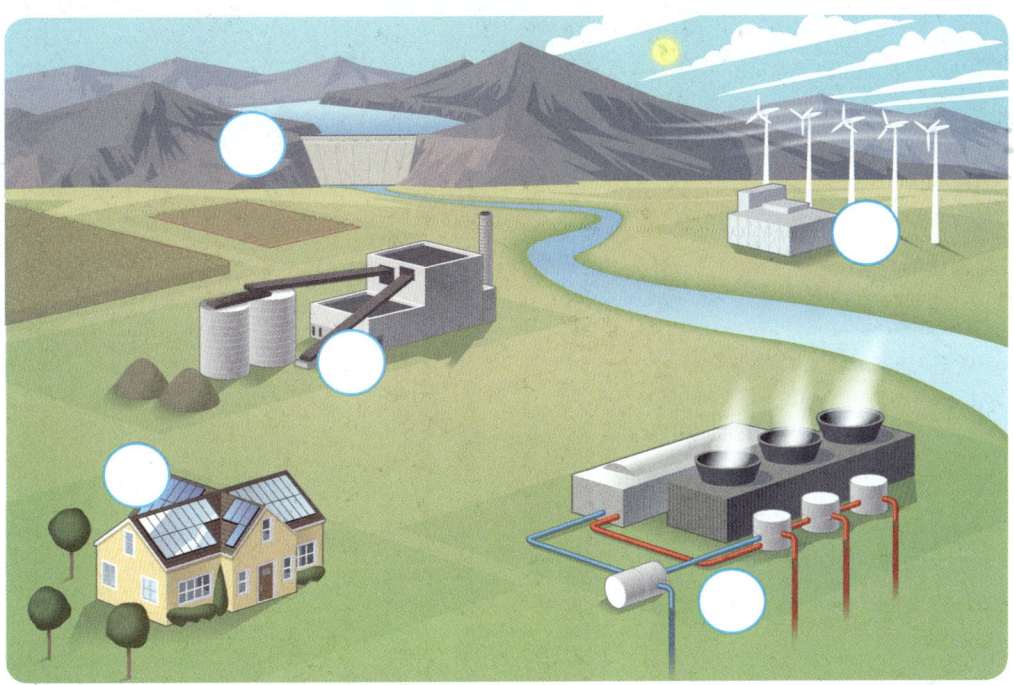

a. Using wind as an energy source does not produce pollution. Because wind will not run out, it is a renewable resource.

b. Geothermal stations use the heat below Earth's surface to produce electricity. Earth's heat is a renewable resource.

c. The energy of water flowing through a dam is called hydroelectricity. Hydroelectric dams use water, which is a renewable resource.

d. Solar energy is renewable energy from the sun. Solar panels capture energy from the sun and change it to electricity, giving off no pollution. Solar energy can also be stored in batteries for later use.

e. Biomass is fuel that comes from dead organisms. The most common type is wood. Other types include cornstalks and animal waste. When burned, biomass is used to generate electricity.

As you've learned, nonrenewable resources cannot be replenished in a reasonable amount of time. **Renewable resources** are resources that can be replenished within a reasonable amount of time. Before the 20th century, people mainly used renewable resources for energy. Renewable resources are now used to generate electricity.

Energy Stations

Explore the images to discover more about forms of renewable energy.

Wind energy does not pollute the air. Wind spins the blades of huge turbines. The spinning blades turn a device called a generator. The generator spins to produce electricity.

Solar energy is clean energy. Each solar panel contains several dozen solar cells. These are devices that turn the sun's energy into electricity.

Geothermal energy is heat from Earth. A geothermal station uses steam from underground to spin the blades of a turbine. The turbine spins a generator that makes an electric current.

Hydroelectric energy is fueled by water, a clean energy source. A hydroelectric station is a dam with machinery inside. Water flows through the dam, turning the blades of a turbine. The turbine then spins a generator, producing electricity.

Making Sense

How does the evidence you gathered about renewable resources help you explain how new technologies allow for new sources of fuel?

EXPLORATION

Pros and Cons
How We Use Resources

The pros and cons of something are similar to its benefits and risks. The pros are the positive things about it, and the cons are the negative things, or *drawbacks*. Fossil fuels have some pros and some cons. A *pro* is that fossil fuels provide affordable fuel. A *con* is that they can cause pollution, harm ecosystems, or produce harmful substances when mixed with water, air, or soil.

Many vehicles run on gasoline. Transporting crude oil sometimes results in hazardous oil spills.

Airplanes use fossil fuel to run their engines. This fuel is expensive and also adds pollution to the air.

Burning fossil fuels in cars and at electricity-generating stations generates energy, but it also causes pollution.

Burning natural gas or using nuclear energy produces less pollution than coal and oil, but transporting uranium is dangerous.

Write the letter of the sentence that completes the chart.

Cause	Effect
	Pollution and harmful gases are added to the air.
New nuclear stations are built.	
	Hazardous oil spills damage environments.

a. Uranium must be moved long distances.
b. Fossil fuels are burned.
c. Crude oil must be transported.

LESSON 3 • Resources 271

Benefits and Drawbacks

The table below shows the benefits and drawbacks of several types of renewable energy. Fill in the source for each type of energy.

> hydroelectric dam   solar panels   wind turbines   geothermal station   biomass station

Source	Benefits	Drawbacks
biomass station	• energy source never runs out • reduces waste that goes in landfills	• can pollute air
hydroelectric dam	• clean energy source • energy source never runs out	• habitat loss • can harm wildlife • floods valuable land • expensive to build or set up
wind turbines	• clean energy source • energy source never runs out	• can harm wildlife • can be noisy and unattractive • only work well on windy days
solar panels	• clean energy source • energy source never runs out	• expensive to build or set up • work better on sunny days
geothermal station	• energy source never runs out	• can be used in a limited number of places • release chemicals that can pollute air • expensive to build or set up

Solar panels, hydroelectric dams, and geothermal stations can be expensive to build or set up. Both wind turbines and hydroelectric dams can harm wildlife. Biomass and geothermal stations may also pollute the air. Hydroelectric dams can cause habitat loss and flood valuable land. However, these renewable energy sources still cause less pollution than nonrenewable resources, and they will never run out.

Explain Match each cause with its effect.

Cause
People think that these can be unattractive and make too much noise.

At times, these can flood valuable land and harm wildlife.

Effect
A community meeting is being held to stop the construction of a hydroelectric dam.

Some people prefer not to install wind turbines.

Hybrid Cars

As you learned, cars need energy to move. Most of this energy comes from oil, the main source of gasoline. Hybrid cars, however, are designed to use two or more methods to generate energy. Some hybrid cars run on both gasoline and electricity. The model shows a standard hybrid.

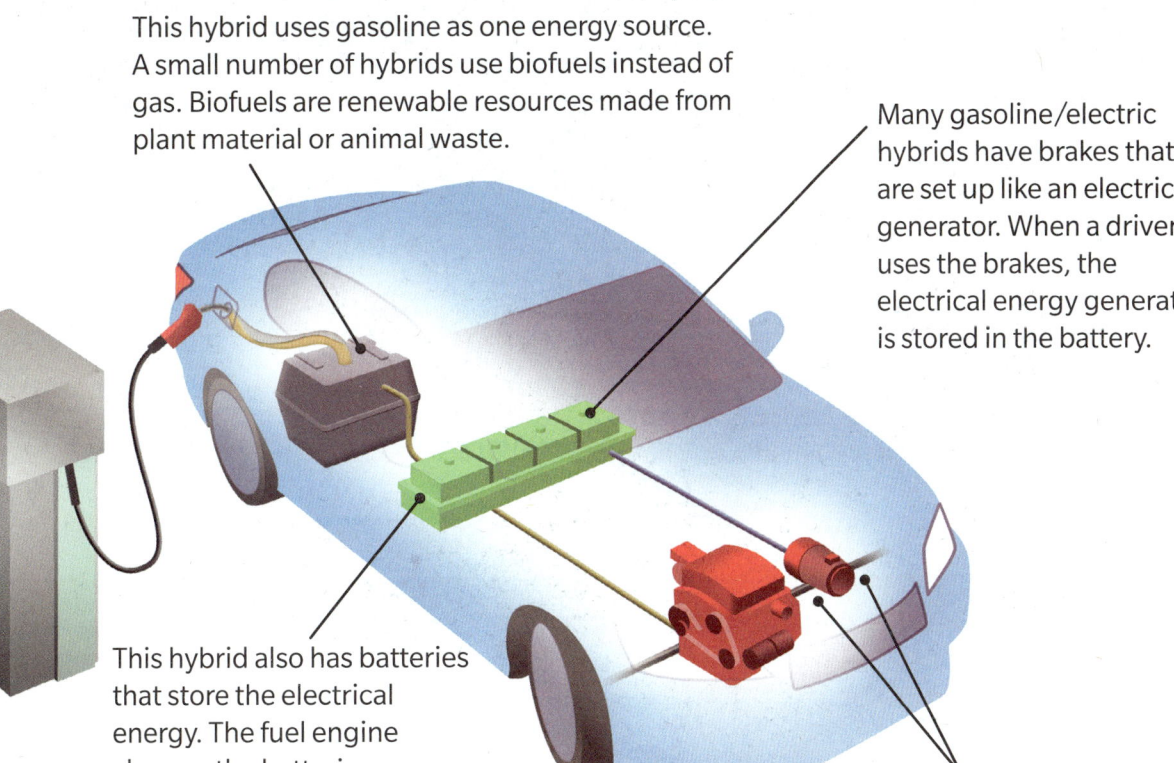

This hybrid uses gasoline as one energy source. A small number of hybrids use biofuels instead of gas. Biofuels are renewable resources made from plant material or animal waste.

Many gasoline/electric hybrids have brakes that are set up like an electric generator. When a driver uses the brakes, the electrical energy generated is stored in the battery.

This hybrid also has batteries that store the electrical energy. The fuel engine charges the batteries.

Most hybrids use a parallel design in which either the gas engine or the electric motor alone can drive the wheels, or they can work at the same time.

In the space below, identify an example of how using nonrenewable resources can affect organisms and their environment.

_____
_____
_____

Going Green Debate

Choosing energy efficiency means using products or technologies that perform the same function but consume less energy. As you have discovered, a compact fluorescent bulb is more energy efficient than a traditional incandescent bulb. It uses much less electrical energy to produce the same amount of light.

How do you think renewable and nonrenewable resources compare? Which one do you think is more energy efficient? Consider both types of energy resources, and then fill out the table below.

- Under *Claim*, fill in either "renewable" or "nonrenewable" to complete the sentence.
- Then under *Evidence*, give three facts that support your claim.
- Use facts from this lesson and the previous one. Research any other facts you need to use as evidence.

Claim
I think that _____ energy is the most efficient type of energy.
Evidence
a. _____
b. _____
c. _____

Making Sense

How does your claim or the evidence you gathered about pros and cons of resource use help you explain how new technologies allow for new sources of fuel?

_____
_____
_____
_____

Name _____

Lesson Check

Can You Explain It?

Think back to the cars from the beginning of the lesson. Now that you've learned about nonrenewable resources, explain how new technologies have allowed cars to use alternative sources of energy. Be sure to do the following:

- Identify the types of fuel sources used for energy.
- Identify technologies that engineers are using to reduce our use of fossil fuels.
- Identify the benefits and drawbacks of at least one renewable resource and one nonrenewable resource.

Now I know or think that _____

_____

_____

_____

Making Connections

When spending time in nature, it can be hard to find sources of energy you can use without disturbing the environment. How does the technology on this backpack allow campers to use new sources of energy?

_____

_____

_____

_____

LESSON 3 • Resources

Checkpoints

1. Write the letter next to the picture of each nonrenewable energy resource that people use as fuel sources.
    a. natural gas
    b. coal
    c. uranium
    d. crude oil

2. Write the words or phrases that make each sentence correct.

| inexpensive | decreasing quickly | increasing quickly |
| increasing slowly | hundreds | hundreds of millions |

Fossil fuels were once easy to find and _____ to use because there was so much of each available. But today, we are using so much that supplies are _____. Because it takes _____ of years for fossil fuels to form, there will be no more when our current supply is gone.

3. Circle the following that result from using fossil fuels.
    a. Air is polluted with harmful gases.
    b. Nonrenewable resources are conserved.
    c. Ecosystems can be harmed.
    d. Renewable resources are all used up.

4. A new electricity-generating station wants to avoid using any nonrenewable energy resources to produce electricity. Which energy resource should the station not use?
    a. geothermal
    b. hydroelectric
    c. natural gas
    d. solar

5. Read the sentences below. Choose the best phrase to complete each sentence.

> it is available everywhere
> it never harms wildlife
> it will never run out
> it produces little or no pollution

There are many benefits to using renewable energy sources. One of the benefits of using a renewable energy source is that _____ . Another benefit is that _____ .

6. Match each cause with its correct effect.

Cause	Effect
Dams are built.	Geothermal stations can release pollution.
Some processes release water that contains chemicals.	Valuable land can be flooded.

7. Choose the correct answer. An electricity-generating station doesn't want to use biomass to produce electricity due to its drawbacks. Which of these is a drawback of using biomass to produce electricity?

  a. It is nonrenewable.
  b. It is very costly to use.
  c. It can be used in few places.
  d. It can produce air pollution.

8. Identify two benefits and two drawbacks of each resource.

Renewable resource	Benefits	Drawbacks
solar		
wind		

LESSON 3 • Resources

Unit Review

Name _____

1. Which fuel source is was caused by once-living plants being buried millions of years ago? Circle the correct choice.

   a. oil
   b. coal
   c. uranium
   d. natural gas

2. Combine information you know and what you have learned to identify what is true of the product sold here. Circle all that apply.

   a. It is a natural resource.
   b. Its use causes pollution.
   c. It is a renewable resource.
   d. It is a nonrenewable resource.

3. Use the word bank and information you've obtained to complete the sentences.

   | renewable energy   nonrenewable energy   solar   wind   fossil fuel |

   A _____ is a useful, concentrated source of energy,

   but is _____. Tidal, _____,

   and _____ energy are _____.

   People's demands for improved technologies causes change, the

   effect of which is more efficient energy sources.

4. Suppose you wanted to move into a wilderness cabin and use only renewable energy sources. What would you need to know about the location? Why?

   _____

   _____

   _____

5. Use the information obtained from the lessons and the word bank below to complete the sentence.

| stored   created   reduced   increased |

Energy from the sun can be _____, the effect of which allows energy to be used when sunlight is unavailable.

6. You develop a new type of electric vehicle. Explain what criteria and constraints you will use to judge the performance of your solution compared to other vehicles.

_____
_____
_____
_____
_____

7. How do natural processes on Earth cause natural hazards such as hurricanes or volcanoes?

_____
_____
_____

8. Looking at this map, if an earthquake happens on land, according to the patterns you explored, where is it most likely to occur?

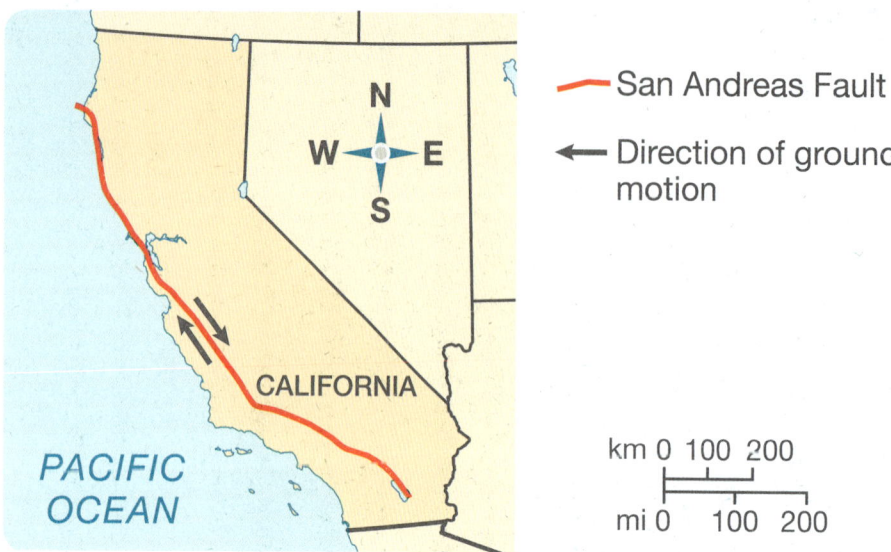

a. along a fault line
b. near the edges of a continent
c. along the mountain ranges of the continent
d. in the center of big cities

9. According to the patterns you explored, where are volcanic eruptions most likely to occur on land?

a. near coasts
b. all over a continent
c. in higher areas such as mountains
d. only in the ocean

10. You learned about several features found on the ocean floor. How do those compare with the ones on land?

a. All of them are found on land.
b. Most of them are found on land.
c. They do not include volcanoes.
d. They do not include mountains.

Interactive Glossary

As you learn about each item, add notes, drawings, or sentences in the extra space. This will help you remember what the terms mean. Here's an example:

fungi (FUHN•jee) A group of organisms that get nutrients by decomposing other organisms.

hongos Un grupo de organismos que obtienen sus nutrientes al descomponer otros organismos.

Mushrooms are a type of fungi.

Glossary Pronunciation Key

With every Glossary term, there is also a phonetic respelling. A phonetic respelling writes the word the way it sounds, which can help you pronounce new or unfamiliar words. Use this key to help you understand the respellings.

Sound	As in	Phonetic Respelling	Sound	As in	Phonetic Respelling
a	bat	(BAT)	oh	over	(OH•ver)
ah	lock	(LAHK)	oo	pool	(POOL)
air	rare	(RAIR)	ow	out	(OWT)
ar	argue	(AR•gyoo)	oy	foil	(FOYL)
aw	law	(LAW)	s	cell	(SEL)
ay	face	(FAYS)		sit	(SIT)
ch	chapel	(CHAP•uhl)	sh	sheep	(SHEEP)
e	test	(TEST)	th	that	(THAT)
	metric	(MEH•trik)		thin	(THIN)
ee	eat	(EET)	u	pull	(PUL)
	feet	(FEET)	uh	medal	(MED•uhl)
	ski	(SKEE)		talent	(TAL•uhnt)
er	paper	(PAY•per)		pencil	(PEN•suhl)
	fern	(FERN)		onion	(UHN•yuhn)
eye	idea	(eye•DEE•uh)		playful	(PLAY•fuhl)
i	bit	(BIT)		dull	(DUHL)
ing	going	(GOH•ing)	y	yes	(YES)
k	card	(KARD)		ripe	(RYP)
	kite	(KYT)	z	bags	(BAGZ)
ngk	bank	(BANGK)	zh	treasure	(TREZH•er)

G1

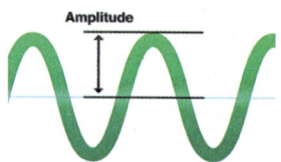

amplitude (AM•pluh•tood) A measure of the amount of energy in a wave. **(p. 135)**

amplitud La mitad de la distancia desde la cresta hasta la depresión de una ola.

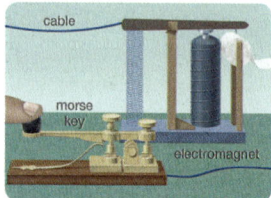

code (KOHD) A system of words, numbers, or other data used in place of other words or letters. **(p. 151)**

código Un sistema de palabras, números u otros datos utilizados en lugar de otras palabras o letras.

circuit (SER•kuht) The closed path or loop that an electric charge flows through. **(p. 94)**

circuito cerrado La trayectoria cerrada o el bucle cerrado a través del cual la carga eléctrica fluye.

collision (kuh•LI•shuhn) The result of two objects bumping into each other. **(p. 119)**

colisión Resultado del choque entre dos objetos.

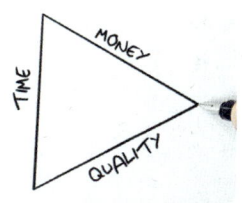

constraint (kuhn•STRAYNT) Something that limits what you are trying to do. **(p. 4)**

restricción Algo que limita lo que se está tratando de hacer.

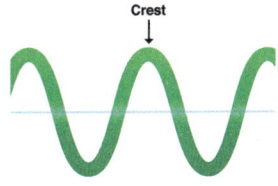

crest (KREST) The top part of a wave. **(p. 135)**

cresta Parte superior de una onda.

criteria (kry•TEER•ee•uh) The desirable features of a solution. **(p. 4)**

criterios Características deseables de una solución

D

deposition (dep•uh•ZISH•uhn) The dropping or settling of eroded materials. **(p. 173)**

deposición Caída o asentamiento de materiales erosionados.

electric current (ee•LEK•trik KER•uhnt) The flow of electric charges along a path. **(p. 97)**

corriente eléctrica Flujo de cargas eléctricas a lo largo de una trayectoria.

energy (EN•er•jee) The ability to do work and cause changes in matter. **(p. 90)**

energía Capacidad de realizar una tarea y causar cambios en la materia.

energy transfer (EN•er•jee TRANZ•fuhr) The movement of energy from place to place or from one object to another. **(p. 99)**

transferencia de eléctrica Movimiento de energía de un lugar a otro o de un objecto a otro.

energy transformation (EN•er•jee TRANZ•fuhr•may•shuhn) A change in energy from one form to another. **(p. 99)**

transformación de la energía Cambio en la energía, de una forma a otra.

engineering (en•juh•NEER•ing) The use of science and math for practical uses such as the design of structures, machines, and systems. **(p. 11)**

ingenieria El uso de las ciencias y las matemáticas para usos prácticos como el diseño de estructuras, máquinas, y sistemas.

environment (en•VEYE•ruhn•muhnt) All the living and nonliving things that surround and affect an organism. **(p. 177)**

medio ambiente Todos los seres vivientes y no vivientes que rodean y afectan a un organismo.

erosion (uh•ROH•zhuhn) The process of moving sediment from one place to another. **(p. 173)**

erosión El proceso de mover el sedimento de un lugar a otro.

fair test (FAYR TEST) To conduct an experiment by changing only one thing at a time making sure all other conditions remain the same. **(p. 16)**

prueba controlada Conducir un experimento donde cambias una cosa a la vez y aseguras que todas las otras condiciones permanecen igual.

G5

fossil (FAHS•uhl) The remains or traces of an organism that lived long ago. **(p. 208)**

fósil Restos o vestigios de un organismo que vivió hace tiempo.

H

heat (HEET) The energy that moves between objects of different temperatures. **(p. 101)**

calor Energía que se mueve entre objetos con temperaturas distintas.

N

natural hazard (NACH•er•uhl HAZ•urd) An earth process that threatens to harm people and property. **(p. 246)**

peligro natural Proceso terrestre que amenaza con dañar a personas y bienes.

natural resource (NACH•er•uhl REE•sawrs) Materials found in nature that people and other living things use. **(p. 266)**

recurso natural Materiales que se encuentran en la naturaleza y que las personas y otros seres vivos utilizan.

nonrenewable resource (nahn•rih•NOO•uh•buhl REE•sawrs) A resource that, once used, cannot be replaced in a reasonable amount of time. **(p. 258)**

recurso no renovable Recurso que, después de haber sido utilizado, no podrá ser reemplazado en un tiempo razonable.

ocean trench (OH•shuhn TRENCH) A long, narrow valley found on the ocean floor. **(p. 230)**

fosa oceánica Un valle largo y angosto que se encuentra en el suelo del océano.

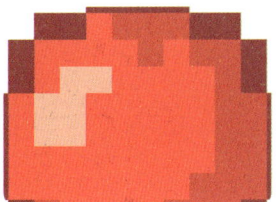

pixel (PIK•suhl) A small unit of color or brightness that when put together with other units form an image. **(p. 147)**

pixel Una pequeña unidad de color o luminosidad que cuando se junta con otras unidades, forma una imagen.

pollution (puh•LOO•shuhn) Waste products that damage an ecosystem. **(p. 267)**

contaminación Todo desperdicio que daña un ecosistema.

prototype (PROH•tuh•typ) An early, usually working, model of a design. **(p. 16)**

prototipo Un modelo de diseño temprano, que generalmente funciona.

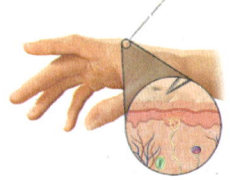

receptors (ree•SEP•turs) Special structures that send information about the environment from different parts of the body to the brain. **(p. 75)**

receptores Estructuras especiales que envían información acerca del ambiente desde distintas partes del cuerpo hacia el cerebro.

relative age (REL•uh•tiv AYJ) The age of one thing compared to another. **(p. 202)**

edad relativa Edad de una cosa al compararla con otra.

renewable resource (rih•NOO•uh•buhl REE•sawrs) A resource that can be replaced within a reasonable amount of time. **(p. 269)**

recurso renovable Recurso que puede ser reemplazado en un tiempo razonable.

 **resource** (REE•sawrs) Any material that can be used to satisfy a need. **(p. 266)**

recurso Cualquier material que pueda ser utilizado para satisfacer una necesidad.

 **senses** (SEN•sez) The way you observe and learn. The five senses are sight, hearing, smell, taste, and touch. **(p. 74)**

sentidos La capacidad de recibir información sobre el ambiente. Los cinco sentidos son la vista, la audición, el olfato, el gusto y el tacto.

 **spore** (SPOR) A reproductive structure of some plants, such as mosses and ferns, that can form a new plant. **(p. 37)**

espora Estructura reproductiva de algunas plantas, como los musgos y los helechos, que puede generar una nueva planta.

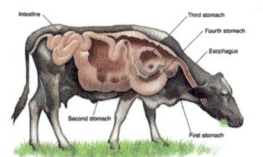 **structure** (STRUK•chur) Something made of parts assembled in a certain way. **(p. 35)**

estructuras Cosas hechas de partes que están ensambladas de cierta manera.

T

technology (tek•NAHL•uh•jee) Engineered products and processes that meet a want or need. **(p. 10)**

tecnología Diseño de productos y procesos que cumplen con una necesidad o un requisito.

trough (TROF) The bottom part of a wave. **(p. 135)**

depresión Parte inferior de una onda.

V

volume (VAHL•yoom) How loud or soft a sound is. **(p. 136)**

volumen Cuán alto o bajo es un sonido.

W

wave (WAYV) The up-and-down movement of surface water. It can also be a disturbance that carries energy through space. **(p. 126)**

ola Movimiento hacia arriba y hacia abajo de la superficie del agua.

onda Alteración que transporta energía a través del espacio.

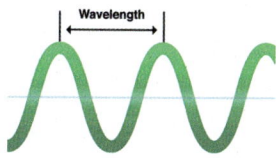

wavelength (WAYV•length) The distance between a point on one wave and the identical point on the next wave. **(p. 135)**

longitud de onda Distancia entre un punto en una onda y ese mismo punto en la próxima onda.

weathering (WETH•er•ing) The breaking down of rocks on Earth's surface into smaller pieces. **(p. 173)**

desgaste Descomposición de las piedras de la superficie terrestre en piezas más pequeñas.

Index

A

adaption to environment, 55
Akaroa Head (New Zealand), 206
ammonites, 208
amplitude, 135–137
animal. *See also* **bird; fish; insect**
   alpaca, 53
   antelope, 47
   attract mates, 50
   bat, 54, 64, 65, 66, 69, 73, 76, 78, 80, 81
   beaver, 178
   behavior, 50–52
   body covering, 52–53
   body parts, 61
   body systems, 58
   cow, 59, 60
   dolphin, 54
   find food, 64, 76
   foods they eat, 46–47
   frog, 47, 52, 54
   giant tube worm, 47
   glass frog, 44, 45, 49, 57, 60, 61
   internal structures, 58–60
   jellyfish, 59, 60
   mammal, 57
   meerkat, 177
   mollusk, 57
   mountain lion, 47
   mouth parts, 47
   polar bear, 52
   porcupine, 53
   reproduction, 50–51, 52, 56
   reptile, 56
   sea cucumber, 53
   snails, 208
   snake, 53
   structures, 45, 46, 57
   structures and behaviors, 45
   structures to move, 54–55
   that do not move, 55
   tortoise, 53
anther, 29
anvil, 79
apple tree, 28, 37
arteries, 58, 60
ash, 228, 230, 247
autumn, 39

B

bark, 37
baseball player, ball, bat, 114
battery, 94–96, 98, 100
benefits and drawbacks, 272, 275
benefits and risks, 267, 271
binary code, 154
biofuel, 273
biomass, 269, 272, 277
biomass station, 272
bird, 53, 56
   chicken, 59, 60
   eagle, 47
   hummingbird, 46
   pigeon, 54
   quetzal, 50
bit, 154
blood, 58, 60
body structures, 70
bones, 74
brain, 74, 75, 77, 79
brainstorm, 15, 17, 18
build a structure, 4
bulb
   fluorescent, 274
   incandescent, 274
buoy, 129, 132, 252

C

Cabrillo National Monument (California), 206
California, 234
   Jacumba Wind Caves, 176
   Kern River, 174

Can You Explain It? 19, 27, 41, 45, 61, 65, 81, 89, 105, 109, 121, 125, 139, 143, 159, 167, 179, 183, 195, 199, 215, 223, 235, 239, 253, 257, 275
Can You Solve It? 3
canyon, 166, 167, 174, 182, 183
   formation, 167, 170, 172, 178, 179, 195
   formed by water, 179
Capitol Reef National Park, 207
car, 256–257, 271, 273
cause and effect, 178, 247
cell phone, 99, 154
   text message, 157
cell phone tower, 157
central nervous system, 74, 75, 83
changes
   fast, 182
   to land shape, 193
   to landforms, 194
   quick, 184, 190, 191
   slow, 182, 184, 190, 192
Checkpoints, 20–21, 42–43, 62–63, 82–83, 106–107, 122–123, 140–141, 160–161, 180–181, 196–197, 216–217, 236–237, 254–255, 276–277
chemical energy, 98, 99, 100
   battery, 98, 99
   coal, 97
choosing energy efficiency, 274
circuit, 94–96
circulatory system, 58, 60
claim, evidence, and reasoning, in Hands-On Activity, 5, 9, 31, 34, 49, 51, 69, 73, 93, 96, 113, 116, 128, 146, 149, 170, 172, 187, 189, 201, 205, 227, 229, 242, 245, 261, 265

I12

coal, 97, 97, 258, 266, 267, 268, 271
cochlea, 79
code, 151, 153
    digital, 154–156
coded message
    flags, 153
    scytale, 153
Colca Canyon, Peru, 174
collision, 119, 121
Colorado plateau, 213
communication
    computer, 156
    drums, 150
    information transfer, 150
    lanterns, 150
    Morse code, 151
    sign language, 144
    smoke signals, 150
    team, 17–18
    telegraph, 151–152
    volleyball team, 17
computer, 100, 154–156
cones, 37
constraint, 4
    identifying, 12, 13
    meeting, 18
    mold solutions, 15
    time, materials, and budget, 17
crash-test dummy, 119
crest, 135
criteria, 4, 263, 265
    identifying, 12, 13
    meeting, 16, 18
    mold solutions, 15
crude oil, 266, 271
    gasoline made from, 268
cypress forest, 211

D

dam, 269, 270, 272
decode, 153
deposition, 173, 176, 178, 192, 212
    speed, 193, 194
depth perception, 78
desert, 177
design process, 12, 13, 18
design solution, 4, 17, 19
designed, 273
device, 90
digestive system, 58, 59
disaster supply kit, 251
drawback, 271
drought, 246, 248, 251

E

ear, 79
    drum, 79
    structures, 79
    trumpet, 14
earthquake, 134, 224, 230, 232, 233, 243, 246, 248, 250, 251
    activity in California, 234
    epicenter, 234
    magnitude, 240
    quick changes, 190
    recorded in rock layers, 213
    resistant building, 249
    wave, 135
    withstanding, 240
Earth's surface
    changes, 171, 172, 173, 174, 177, 178, 183, 184, 187, 189, 190, 191, 192, 194, 212, 215
    factors that shape, 166, 179, 195
    processes that affect, 246
echolocation, 80
egg, 29
    animal, 56, 57
electric circuit, 10
electric current, 97
electrical energy, 97, 98, 99, 100, 268, 274
    batteries store, 273

electricity
    from nonrenewable resources, 258, 266, 268
    run hybrid cars, 273
email message, 155–156
encode, 153
energy, 92
    change, 98, 99
    chemical, 97, 100
    comes from, 97
    devices, 92
    electrical, 97, 98, 100, 268
    forms of, 98
    generation, 271
    geothermal, 270
    heat, 99, 101
    heat transfer, 101–102
    hydroelectric, 270
    less, 119
    light, 97, 98, 99
    more, 119
    motion, 98, 99, 117, 131
    nuclear, 266, 271
    pros and cons, 271
    renewable, 270
    solar, 269, 270
    sound, 97, 98, 99, 103, 131
    sources, 261, 265, 269, 270, 272, 275
    and speed, 118
    stations, 270
    stored, 97, 100, 117, 230
    sun, 97, 262
    transfer, 99, 100, 104, 110, 114, 131
    transfer and transform, 89, 105
    transformation, 98, 99, 120
    using, 90
    vibration, 103
    wind, 270
energy efficient, 274
engineer, 239, 249, 253, 275

Index

design process, 12
identify a problem, 13
improve and test phase, 17
improve existing design, 14
make and test, 15
mechanical, 11
role in technology, 10
solve problems, 4, 12
test and retest design, 16
engineering, 11
design process, 13, 18
team, 17
enhance hearing, 19
environment, 39, 52, 177, 211
erosion, 173, 174, 179, 187, 195
forces, 178
rate of, 192
in rock layers, 212, 213
speed, 193, 194
wind, 176
eruption, 190, 228, 229, 230, 247
Exploration
Bits and Bytes, 154–158
Body Building, 52–57
Collisions, 119–120
Earth's Surface, 173–178
Energy Is All Around, 97–100
Energy of Sound, 103–104
Evidence of Environments, 208–214
Exploring Renewable Resources, 269–270
Fast Changes, 190–191
Finding Patterns, 232–234
Heat, 100–101
History of Information Transfer, 150–153
How Engineers Solve Problems, 12–18
How Plants Change, 39–40
How Waves Transfer Energy, 131–134
Inside Out, 58–60
By Land or By Sea, 230–231
Layers of Rock, 206–207
Materials We Use, 266–268
Natural Hazard Solutions, 249–252
Natural Hazards, 246–248
Plant Structures Have Special Functions, 35–38
Pros and Cons, 271–274
Sights and Sounds, 77–80
Slow Changes, 192–194
Things That Move Have Energy, 117–118
Too Hot to Handle! 120
Touchy Feely, 74–76
Wave Parts, 135–138
What is Engineering? 10–11
explore phase, 12, 18
explosion, 243
eye, 77, 78
structures, 77

fair test, 16
fast changes, 182, 190
fault (Earth surface), 214
fibrous root, 36
filament, 27
fish, 56, 208
parrot fish, 61
shark, 54, 59, 60
flashlight, 94, 98
flood, 182, 191, 246, 248, 251
flooding, erosion, 174
flower, 28, 37
parts, 29, 29, 37
fluorescent bulb, 274
food-carrying tubes, 38
footprint on a rock wall, 198, 205, 207, 214, 215
force, 119

forces
change Earth's surface, 173, 184
earthquake, 214
in rocks, 213
fossil fuels, 266, 267, 271, 275
fossils, 208, 209, 212, 215
in rock layers, 214
freshwater lake, 211
fruit, 27, 28, 31, 34, 37, 38, 40, 41
fuel, 266, 268, 269
sources for energy, 275

gasoline, 268, 271, 273
geothermal station, 269, 272
giant wave, 248
glacier, 188, 189, 192
going green, 274
Grand Canyon (Arizona), 213
gravity, erosion, 173
green stem, 36
growth, 36

H

hammer, 79, 120
Hands-On Activity
Bobbing and Waving, 129–130
Engineer It • Communication Solution, 144–146
Courtship Displays, 50–51
Dinner is Served, 46–49
Engineer It • Designing a Listening Device, 6–9
Flower Power, 28–31
Full of Energy, 90–93
Glaciers on the Move, 188–189
Layer by Layer, 202–205
Let's Make Waves, 126–128, 200–201
Light the Bulb, 94–96

I14

Make Your Own Seismograph, 243–245
Modeling Energy Resource Use, 258–261
Modeling How Far Sediment Travels, 168–170
No Smell, No Taste, No See, 70–73
Pixels to Pictures, 147–149
Engineer It • Quick Tower Building, 4–5
The Rate of Change, 184–187
Engineer It • Running on Sunshine, 262–265
Slurp! 32–34
Speed and Energy, 114–116
Engineer It • Strong, Stable Structures, 240–242
A Sweet Test, 171–172
Test It! Stored Energy in a Rubber Band, 110–113
Touch Test, 66–69
Tracking Quakes, 224–227
Volcanic Eruptions, 228–229

hearing, 2
   enhanced device, 6, 14

hearing receptor, 79
heart, 58, 60
heat, 266
   energy transfer, 101–102
   from nonrenewable resources, 258

high definition (HD), 158
hike, 6
hurricane, 191, 246, 248, 251
hybrid car, 273
   design, 273

hydroelectric dam, 272
hydroelectricity, 269

I

ice, 175
improve and test phase, 17, 18
incandescent bulb, 274

information transfer, 159
   drums, 150
   lanterns, 150
   smoke signals, 150

inner ear, 79
insect, 56
   ant, 54
   mosquito, 47
   peacock spider, 50
   termite, 178

internal structures, animal, 58–60

L

land formation, 223, 231, 234
landform
   change, 168, 171
   rock layers, 200, 202

landslide, 184, 190, 243, 246, 248, 250, 252
larvae, 56
lava, 190, 230
   formation, 228

leaves, 35, 36
   change color, 39

Lesson Check, 19, 41, 61, 81, 105, 121, 139, 159, 179, 195, 215, 235, 253, 275

light reflection, 78
light wave, 133
listening device, 3, 5, 6, 9, 11, 18, 19
listening post, 14
liver, 58
living and nonliving things, 177
living things
   change Earth's surface, 178
   change environment, 177

local area network (LAN), 156
lungs, 58

M

make and test phase, 15, 18
Making Sense, in Hands-On Activity, 5, 9, 11, 18, 31, 34, 38, 40, 49, 51, 57, 60, 69, 73, 76, 80, 93, 96, 100, 102, 104, 113, 116, 118, 120, 128, 130, 134, 138, 146, 149, 153, 158, 170, 172, 178, 187, 189, 191, 194, 201, 205, 207, 214, 227, 229, 231, 234, 242, 245, 248, 252, 261, 265, 268, 270, 274

map, 222, 223, 227, 229, 231, 235
   to find patterns, 235
   helping people see patterns, 235
   ocean floor, 231, 232
   volcanos and earthquakes, 233

mechanical engineer, 11
mechanical part, 10
message, 151–153
   decode, 153
   encode, 153
   flags, 153
   scytale, 153

middle ear, 79
molten rock, 228, 247, 252
Morse, Samuel, 151
Morse code, 151–152
motion energy, 117, 131
mountain, 233
   formation, 230

mudslide, 190, 193
multibeam sonar, 231
muscles, 76
music, 89

N

natural gas, 266, 268, 271
natural hazard, 246
   affect people, 248
   cause and effect, 247, 248
   drought, 246, 247
   earthquake, 246, 247
   flood, 246, 248

Index

hurricane, 246, 247
impacts of, 239
landslide, 246, 247
making plans for, 250
patterns, 250, 251
reducing the impacts of, 245, 252, 253
solutions, 249, 253
tsunami, 246, 248
volcano, 246, 247
wildfire, 246, 247
natural resource, 266
needles (evergreen), 36
nerves, 74, 75, 79
nervous system, 74, 75
nonrenewable resource, 266, 274, 275
collecting, 268
costs and benefits, 258
found, 267
processing, 268
used for electricity, 258
used for heat, 258
nuclear energy, 266, 271

O

ocean floor, 230
mountain, 231
pattern, 232
trench, 231
volcano, 231
ocean trench, 230, 232
oil, 271
outer ear, 79
ovary, 29
ovule, 29

P

Paria Canyon, 176
part of a flower
female, 29
male, 29
pattern, 230
on Earth, 227, 229, 231, 234

of earthquakes, 224, 234
of ground movement, 250
on land, 233
of land formations, 223
on a map, 235
on the ocean floor, 232
in rock, 176
in rock colors, 207
of rock layers, 212, 213
of weather and climate, 251
petal, 29, 37
pistil, 29
pixel, 147, 158
plant
apple tree, 26
behaviors, 40
cacti, 37
evergreen tree, 36
fern, 37, 208
flower, 28
ivy, 178
needs, 32, 35
parts, 35
respond to light, 40
response to gravity, 40
roots, 32, 177
rose, 37
slow changes to Earth, 192
stem, 32
structures, 35, 36, 38, 39, 41
survive, grow, reproduce, 27
tree, 27, 31, 34, 38, 40
pole vaulter, 110
pollen, 28, 29, 37
pollination, 28
pollution, 271
precipitation, 177
prints, 215
on a rock wall, 199, 201
protection, 36
prototype, 16, 18

Q

quick changes, 184, 190, 191.

See also **fast changes**

R

radio waves, 157
rain, 174, 193
rain forest, 177
receptors, 75, 76
reflex, 76
relative age, 202
of rock layers, 206
renewable energy, 270
benefits and drawbacks, 272
renewable resources, 269, 274, 275
biofuel, 273
reproduction, 36
animal, 50, 56
eggs, 56
structures, 56
resolution, high definition (HD), 158
resource, 266
respiratory system, 58
Ring of Fire, 233
ripples, 131
river, 172, 173, 179
of ice, 188, 192
rock, 168, 173, 200
bridge, 179
forces, 213
formation, 207, 212, *212*, 213
wall, 198, 199, 201, 205, 207, 214, 215
rock layer, 200, 201, 211, 213, 215
bends, 214
differs, 207
earthquake motion recorded in, 213
fossils, 209, 210, 214
make landforms, 202
pattern, 212, 213
record landform changes, 198

relative age, 206
thickness, 207
roots, 35, 40, 177
absorb, 38
take in water and minerals, 32

S

saltwater sea, 211
San Andreas Fault, 235
sand, 176, 194
sand dune, 168, 173, 176
satellite, 132, 142–143, 153
scientist, 239
scytale, 153
sea arch, 171
seasonal change, 39, 41
sediment, 168, 170, 173, 192
seed, 29, 37
seismic wave, 134
detect and measure, 243
seismograph, 243, 252
semicircular canal, 79
senses, 74, 80
air over bat's wings, 66
body, 75
to find food, 69, 73
five, 81
inside a nose, 70
smell, 70
sensory receptor, 77
sensory structure, 66
sepal, 29
Sierra Nevada mountains, 173
sight, 77
signal, 155–156
electronic, 154
satellite, 154
skeletal system, 74
skin, 66, 75
skin sensory structure, 66
slow changes, 182, 184, 190, 192
smell, 70

soil erosion, 36
solar energy, 269
solar heater, 262
solar panel, 269, 272
solutions to problems, 14
solve problems, 4, 12, 15, 18, 19
sound
energy, 103, 133, 135–137
enhancement, 14
loud, 104
matter, 133
soft, 104
traveling, 133
vibration, 79, 80, 103
waves, 103, 133, 136–137, 157, 231
sound-system, 16
speed of change, 193
spinal cord, 74, 76
spines, 37
spores, 37
stamen, 29, 37
stems, 35, 38, 40
stethoscope, 14
stirrup, 79
stomach, 58
Stoney Creek (Ontario), 206
stored energy, 100, 230
structure, 35, 41
structures
body, 70
smell, 70
sunlight, 35, 39, 40
surfer, 124, 125
system, 58

T

taproot, 36
taste, 70
taste buds, 70
technology, 10
new, 275
new energy sources, 261, 265

new fuel sources, 257, 268, 270, 274
new or improve, 11
nonrenewable resource, 267
reducing impacts of natural hazards, 252
telegraph, 151–152
temperature, 101
test and retest design, 16
text message, 153, 155
The Alps, 206
thorns, 37
tiltmeter, 252
trench, 230
trough, 135
tsunami, 246, 248, 251, 252

U

underwater
mountain range, 232
volcano, 232
Unit Review, 22–24, 84–86, 162–164, 218–220, 278–280
uranium, 266, 268, 271

V

veins, 58, 60
vision, 78
volcanic eruption, 247, 248, 250
volcano, 230, 232, 233, 243, 246
erupting, 190, 228, 250
lava formation, 228
underwater, 232
volleyball team, 17
volume, 136

W

want or need, 4
meeting, 10, 11, 12, *12*
water
changes Earth's surface, 172, 174, 177

Index

changes landforms, 171
erosion, 174
processes, 193
weathering, 174
water-carrying tubes, 38
wave, 125, 126, 129
    earthquake. *See also* **earthquake**; **seismic wave**
    energy, 133, 134, 141
    erosion, 174, 193
    matter movement, 132, 135
    ocean, 131, 138
    ripples, 131
    sound. *See also* **sound, waves**

wave parts, 139
    amplitude, 135
    crest, 135
    trough, 135
    wavelength, 135
wavelength, 135–138
weathering, 173, 176, 178, 179, 195, 212, 213
    speed, 193, 194
wildfire, 246, 248, 250
willow tree, 211
wind, 170, 269
    changes landforms, 168
    deposition, 173
    energy, 270
    erosion, 173, 176

wind turbines, 272
wings, 66
wire, 97
wireless technology, 154
woody stem, 36
wrecking ball, 108, 109, 121

COLOR Me! Life Science robot

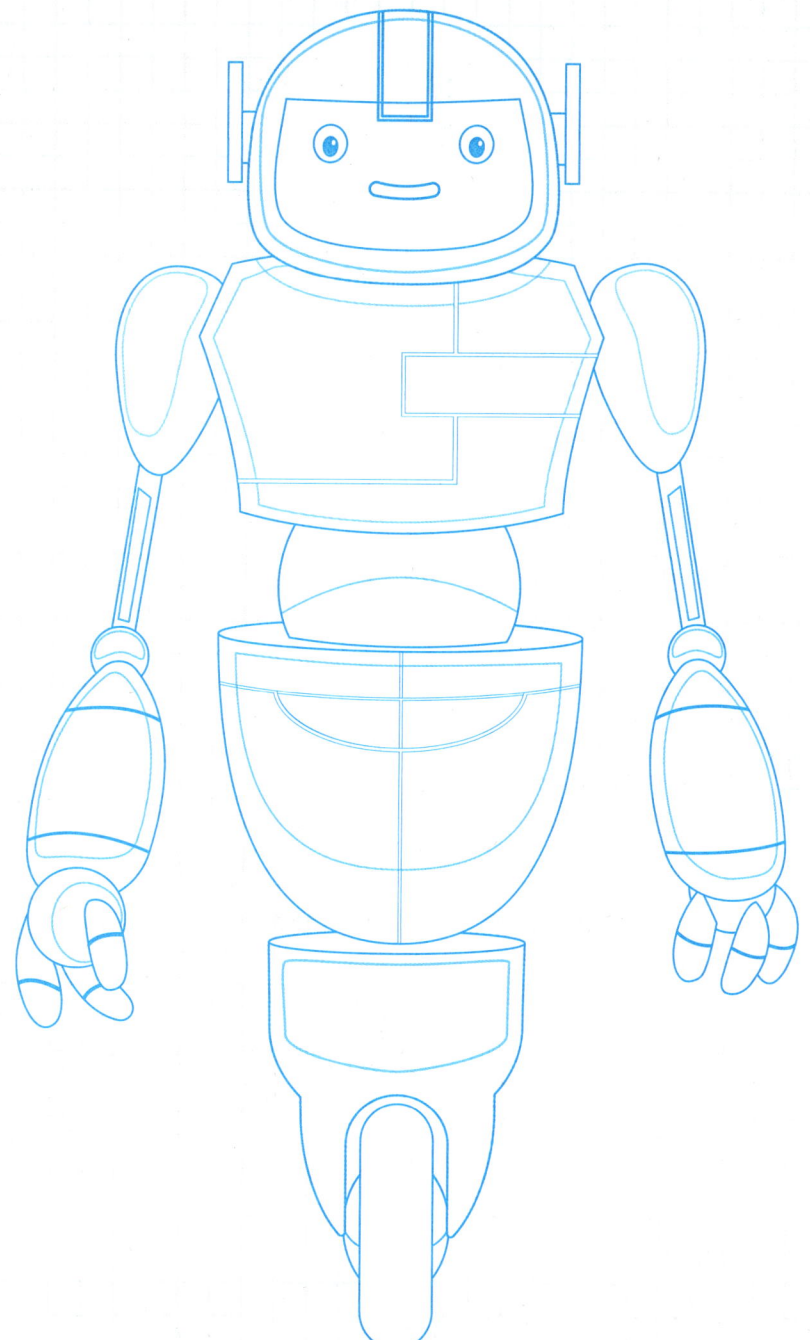

Science is COOL!

COLOR Me! Physical Science robot

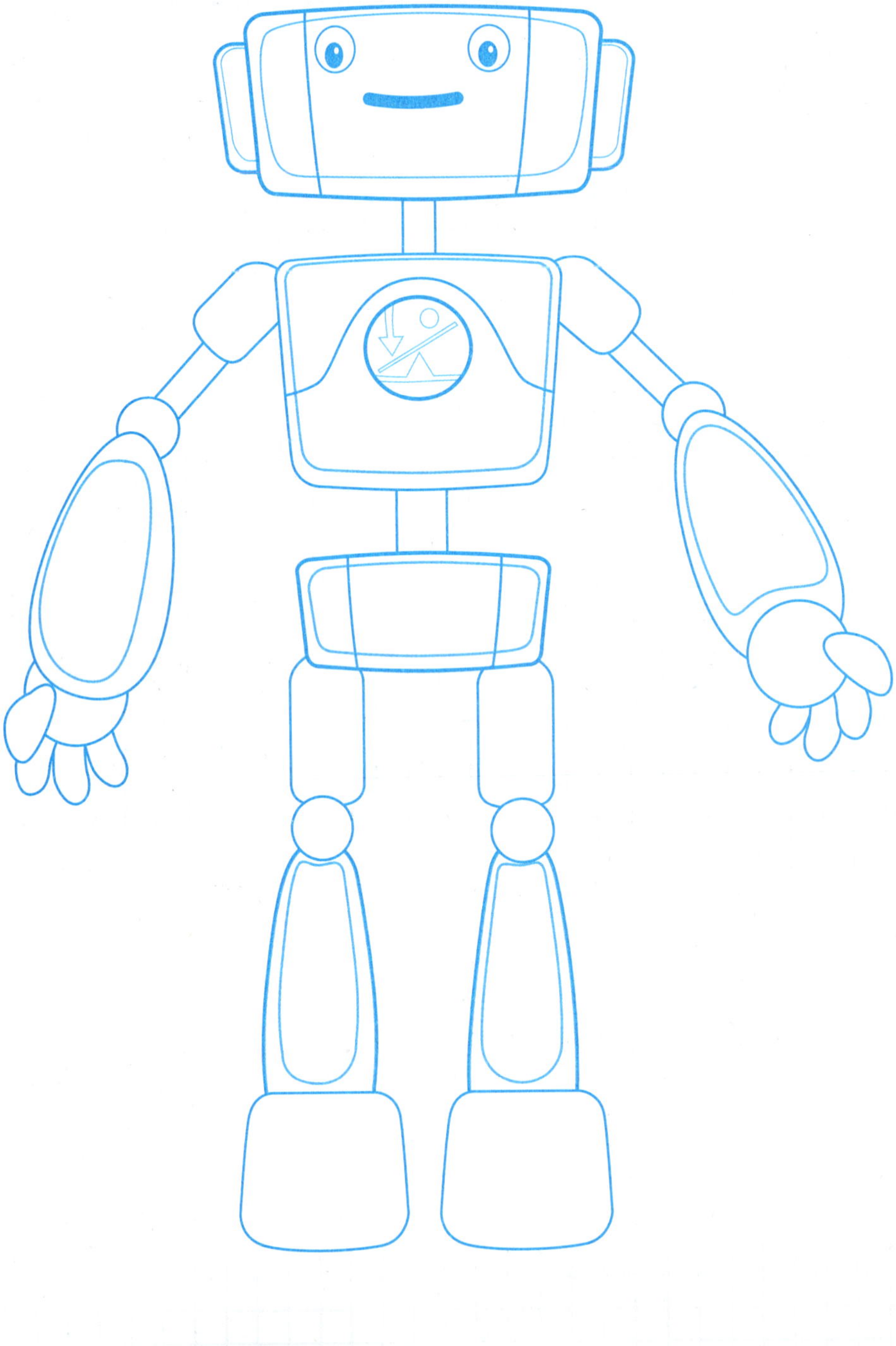

Science is FUN!

COLOR Me! Engineering robot

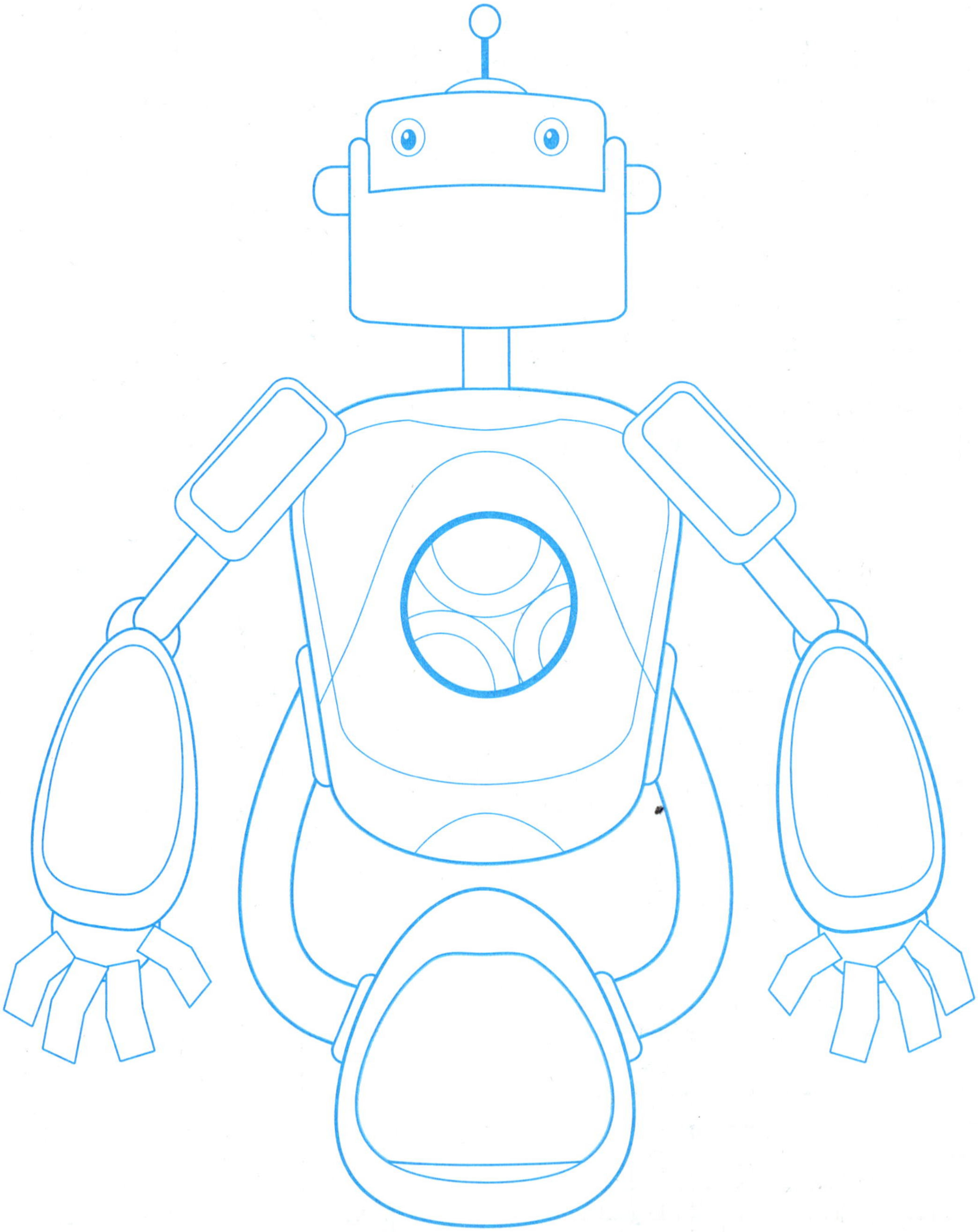

I am a scientist.